The Working Life

The Working Life

The Labor Market for Workers in Low-Skilled Jobs

Nan L. Maxwell

2006

W.E. Upjohn Institute for Employment Research
Kalamazoo, Michigan

Library of Congress Cataloging-in-Publication Data

Maxwell, Nan L.
   The working life : the labor market for workers in low-skilled jobs / Nan L. Maxwell.
      p. cm.
   Includes bibliographical references and index.
   ISBN-13: 978-0-88099-297-8 (pbk. : alk. paper)
   ISBN-10: 0-88099-297-2 (pbk. : alk. paper)
   ISBN-13: 978-0-88099-298-5 (hardcover : alk. paper)
   ISBN-10: 0-88099-298-0 (hardcover : alk. paper)
   1. Unskilled labor—Supply and demand—United States. 2. Labor market—United
States. I. Title.
   HD5724.M339 2006
   331.7'980973—dc22

                              2006032517

© 2006
W.E. Upjohn Institute for Employment Research
300 S. Westnedge Avenue
Kalamazoo, Michigan 49007-4686

Cover design by Alcorn Publication Design.
Index prepared by Nairn Chadwick.
Printed in the United States of America.
Printed on recycled paper.

Contents

Tables

Preface

Virtually everyone starts his or her work life in a low-skilled job and, in an ideal world, everyone advances in career-ladder fashion as that person learns new skills. Not all beginnings are the same, however. Some individuals cannot find an entry into the labor market, while others move seamlessly into the labor force. Some individuals start their work life in low-skilled and fairly mundane positions, while others, like college professors, start their work life in relatively high-skilled positions. Not all endings are the same, either. Some individuals have a work life filled with career moves and a series of progressively higher paying jobs. Others face a lifetime of low-wage, dead-end jobs.

From a policy perspective, individuals that have difficulty moving into an entry-level job or those that are confined to a series of low-wage, dead-end jobs are of concern because they often face a lifetime of low earnings. Labor market difficulties, low earnings, and low levels of skills often go hand in hand with poverty, reliance on government safety nets, and a lifetime of struggling to stay afloat economically. Policy discussions focused heavily on these issues in the 1980s, when rising levels of inequality widened the gap in economic conditions between those in the bottom and those in the top quintile of the income distribution. During the 1990s, the federal government directed three major policies at the problems facing low-wage individuals:

- In 1994, the School-to-Work Opportunities Act (STWOA) focused federal educational policy on building both academic and workplace skills in high schools so students that enter the workforce after high school have the skills necessary to succeed.

- In 1996, the Personal Responsibility and Work Opportunity Reconciliation Act (PRWORA) replaced welfare entitlements with Temporary Assistance for Needy Families (TANF). TANF programs helped welfare recipients make the transition into the workplace, mainly by bolstering their work readiness skills to enable them to move quickly into the labor market.

- In 1998, the Workforce Investment Act (WIA) consolidated employment and training services to streamline training for youth, the unemployed, and displaced workers in an attempt to better their labor market outcomes.

Although the plight of low-skilled workers flits in and out of the public eye, their struggle for economic survival remains a constant. The nature of the struggle may have changed as our economy evolved from an agrarian to a manufacturing to a service base, and as the need for skills shifted from physical (in farming) to mental abilities (in a postindustrial society). Today, as this study shows, obtaining an entry-level, low-skilled job and succeeding in it depends on an ability to execute successfully a relatively wide variety of skills. Moreover, advancing from the entry-level, low-skilled job—in either pay or career progression—requires the worker to expand the initial skill base.

This study examines the labor market that workers face when they compete for a low-skilled job. Its focus is on jobs requiring no more than a high school education and no more than one year of work experience. Using information from 405 employers on their low-skilled positions, we focus on the characteristics and skills that individuals need to obtain, succeed in, and advance from an entry-level position. Our focus on skill requirements increases our understanding of the human capital needed by workers in low-skilled jobs and, as a result, provides policymakers and program managers with insights about the policies and programs needed to build a successful work life for individuals who have little formal education or work experience.

A small army of individuals worked tirelessly to make this study possible and to ensure that errors in the data collection and analysis were virtually nonexistent. Despite their best efforts, errors remain and rest squarely on my shoulders. Everyone involved in the project cannot be duly acknowledged. Indeed, more than 1,270 individuals spent at least a half hour of their time responding to a survey used in our data analysis. Still, several individuals and organizations were critical to success at some juncture of the project's unfolding.

Brian Murphy and Gilbert Robinson, who were then part of the Urban Institute at San Francisco State University, initiated the study by securing funding from the Department of Human Services in San Francisco County for the first rounds of the Employer Survey. Brendan Leung extended the surveying across the bay to Alameda County by securing funding from the Rockefeller Foundation. Monies from the U.S. Department of Housing and Urban Development further expanded the data collection in Alameda County, extended the surveying into San Joaquin County, and added the Household Survey component. The W.E. Upjohn Institute for Employment Research provided funding to round out data collection. The South Hayward Neighborhood Collaborative structured and guided the Household Survey, provided a field office, and gave access to individuals using community-based social services, all of which greatly enriched the study.

A cadre of workers spent countless hours collecting data from employers. Aude Frédérique Sanchez spent three years phoning firms for interviews, visiting 223 of the 405 firms and verifying and organizing the data into readable files. Kami Huntzinger set the stage for surveying employers by her meticulous combing of the literature on skills and by her piloting of surveys, training of surveyors, and building of databases. Dave Marcyes moved across the country for a summer to conduct the Employer Survey in San Joaquin County. Susan Gonzales and Tanisha Fernandez conducted most of the surveys in San Francisco County with help from Svetlana Smirnova. Luis Molina helped conduct surveys in Alameda County. Aashish Bhalla, Shanu Bharagaua, Stephen Fontana, Srinath Kenshau, Flora Kuo, Shanheen Lokandwala, Rebecca Ma, Chrissy Michalski, Shuja Mirza, George Nguyen, Anastassia Ovtchinnikova, Kaushik Ray, Kerry Redmond, Vera Romenskaya, Esra Seynur, Rima Shah, Fiony Tong, and Greg Wright spent countless hours calling employers to set up interviews. Andriy Gostik, Hellen Mbugua, and Mikhail Nekorystnov entered and verified data. Judith Schaefer provided administrative oversight throughout the surveying in Alameda and San Joaquin counties.

Another set of workers pounded the pavement to interview residents in South Hayward. Andé Brescia Peña tirelessly gathered input from the community for the Household Survey and oversaw its piloting. She recruited and trained surveyors, worked with translators to ensure the accuracy of the Spanish version of the survey, managed the field work and administered surveys when needed. Aude Frédérique Sanchez maintained the integrity of the data through verification, provided database management, trained and supervised surveyors, and administered surveys when needed. Jesus Manajarrez provided leadership in conducting the Household Survey, drawing upon his knowledge of the neighborhoods and his bilingual capabilities in administering 187 surveys. Adriana Tello administered 181 surveys in both English and Spanish and provided data entry on the majority of other surveys. Julio Abad, Javier Ochoa, Milagro Rodriguez, and Rocio Tello used their bilingual abilities to administer surveys. Coreena Pai-Rao Chen and Debbie Ohel Jones administered surveys in English, and Debbie provided administrative leadership in setting up and piloting surveys. Masters-level economics students in the Research Methods course at California State University, East Bay, during Spring 2002 each surveyed 13 households. Judith Schaefer provided administrative support for the surveying, and Chao Cong verified data entry.

Yu Liu, Atanas Maximov, Coreena Pai-Rao Chen, Stilyana Salakova, Aude Frédérique Sanchez, and Jian Wu provided research assistance in table construction, verification, or literature review. The study benefited greatly from extensive discussions with Ronald D'Amico, David Neumark, and Lynn Paringer. D'Amico read (and reread) early drafts of the monograph and provided comments that created a firmer foundation for its structure. Dan Hamermesh and Barry Hirsch made comments on early drafts of the study that improved its structure and emphasis. Anonymous referees provided insights and suggestions that strengthened the monograph's flow, presentation, and arguments. Kevin Hollenbeck of the Upjohn Institute offered continual support and greatly improved the monograph with his suggestions and comments, and Benjamin Jones enhanced its readability with his meticulous editing. Erika Jackson typeset the manuscript and tables.

Finally, last in acknowledgment but first in every other way, Ronald and Abigail D'Amico, my husband and daughter, suffered through my frequent mental and physical absences as I fretted over data collection, analysis, and writing. They define life and improve the quality of my work with their foci on walking dogs, going to ball games, and smelling the roses.

1
Low-Skilled Jobs
The Reality behind the Popular Perceptions

My first job, I was 17 years old. I start[ed] working as a nurse's assistant in a hospital. Under my care I had 12 patients. Their lives were in my hands.
   —A low-wage worker

Individuals that work full time spend about 20 percent of their year—and nearly one-third of their waking hours—at work. Individuals have some control over this time, in that they can invest in skills that help shape their work life. Hate working in an office? Build construction skills. Want to help people? Build social interaction skills.

Unfortunately, investing in the skills necessary to get your job of choice is not foolproof, as the market for skills is governed by the laws of supply and demand. These economic forces shape an individual's work life by determining employment probabilities, wages, and potential for career progression.

Most individuals toiling in the labor market focus heavily on the outcomes of labor demand and supply forces. They see their wages as being too low, leaving them without the ability to achieve the life to which they aspire. While virtually all workers voice such complaints, workers in jobs requiring relatively few skills have special concerns, for their wages frequently will not keep their family out of poverty. Perhaps because full-time work may not afford a middle-class lifestyle for workers in low-skilled jobs, questions arise as to whether or not demand and supply forces are fair. How fair is it that some workers must face a life of struggle as they precariously balance full-time work, home responsibilities, and subsistence-level economic needs (DeParle 2004; Munger 2002)?

This book tells the story of the low-skilled jobs available to workers with little formal education or work experience. In the process of telling the story, we debunk several popular perceptions about how the labor

1

market for workers in low-skilled jobs operates. Frequently, this labor market is portrayed as one in which an excess supply of job seekers competes for relatively few jobs (Newman 1999), and in which employers maintain unrealistic employment criteria even when faced with labor shortages (Jasinowski 2001). Because employers (supposedly) can easily find workers, low-skilled jobs are thought to turn into low-wage, dead-end positions.

When we surveyed employers and asked them about their low-skilled positions, they provided a dramatically different description of the labor market and led us to very different conclusions about its operation. Most importantly, employers told us that the labor market for workers in low-skilled jobs is a market for skills. Specifically, they made the following points:

Low-skilled jobs require skills. Low-skilled jobs are not the same as no-skilled jobs, they said. Most jobs require English, math, problem-solving, and communication skills, the so-called new basic skills. More than three-fourths of low-skilled jobs require oral and written comprehension of English, more than half require oral and written expression and deductive reasoning, and at least half require math, reading comprehension, active listening, writing, and speaking. Workers in low-skilled jobs are expected to act appropriately at work and to perceive cues from others correctly. Many low-skilled jobs also require physical abilities and mechanical skills. In fact, low-skilled jobs require physical and mechanical skills at higher levels than other jobs.

Shortages of appropriately skilled workers in low-skilled jobs exist, even when labor markets are slack. Close to 60 percent of the firms in the local labor market in this study had difficulty—one-fourth of them had extreme difficulty—finding qualified workers for low-skilled jobs when unemployment rates exceeded 7.0 percent.

Skills are rewarded in the labor market for workers in low-skilled jobs. Firms increase wages in low-skilled jobs that require skills the firms have difficulty obtaining. Specifically, low-skilled jobs requiring skills with a high relative demand in the local labor market (i.e., skills in short supply) carry increased occupational wages.

Low-skilled jobs offer promotional opportunities. Over 90 percent of entry-level, low-skilled jobs have promotional opportunities. Firms structure promotional opportunities for workers in the entry-level, low-skilled job by requiring workers to expand their abilities to encompass the skill sets used in the job above entry level. The modal title of the position above entry level is lead, supervisor, or manager. Even though entry-level jobs require English and problem-solving skills, jobs above entry-level require higher-level skills in each of these areas.

Hiring requirements in low-skilled jobs are relaxed in tight labor markets. Firms match recruiting and screening methods to the skills needed in the low-skilled job. As labor markets loosen, firms use less extensive recruiting methods—as might be expected with greater numbers of applicants—but adopt more intensive screening methods. The increased screening during loose labor markets suggests that firms sift through the greater number of applicants in order to uncover workers with the skill sets needed in the job.

WHAT ARE LOW-SKILLED JOBS?

We define low-skilled jobs as those requiring workers to have no more than a high school education and no more than one year of work experience. We posit that such jobs are low-skilled by virtue of their limited entrance requirements. Indeed, when we asked firms about education and work requirements for such jobs, about 25 percent stated that there were no educational requirements, and just over 40 percent required no work experience. Only about 30 percent of the positions required that the worker speak, understand, and read English "extremely well."

We characterize low-skilled jobs using both national and local databases.[1] One clear characterization that emerges from the data is that low-skilled jobs are concentrated in a few industries and occupations (Table 1.1). Under the Industry category, the service sector houses nearly 40 percent of low-skilled jobs (and about 37 percent of all jobs). Services, retail trade, and manufacturing together house 75 percent of the low-skilled jobs but only 68 percent of all jobs nationwide. Services

Table 1.1 Industrial and Occupational Distribution of Low-Skilled Jobs

	All jobs	Low-skilled jobs
Industry		
Services	36.7	39.8
Education and medical	16.4	14.2
Business services	10.6	11.0
Other services	9.8	14.6
Retail trade	16.6	22.0
Manufacturing	14.7	13.2
Wholesale trade	4.0	6.5
Finance, insurance, and real estate	6.5	5.8
Public administration	4.4	5.2
Transportation, communication, public utilities	7.2	4.1
Construction	7.0	2.7
Agriculture/mining	2.8	0.8
Occupation		
Office and administrative support	7.3	41.3
Production	14.5	11.1
Food preparation and serving	2.1	9.8
Sales and related	2.7	8.5
Building and grounds cleaning/maintenance	1.2	7.6
Transportation and material moving	6.8	7.1
Personal care and service	4.3	2.8
Installation, maintenance, and repair	6.9	2.1
Education, training, and library	7.5	1.9
Protective service	2.6	1.7
Construction and extraction	7.5	1.2
Health-care support	1.9	1.1
Health-care practitioner/technical	6.0	0.6
Business and financial	3.6	0.5
Farming, fishing, and forestry	1.7	0.5
Computer and mathematical	2.1	0.4
Community and social services	1.8	0.4
Art, design, entertainment, sports, and media	4.8	0.4
Management	3.9	0.3
Architecture and engineering	4.5	0.1
Military	0.0	0.1

Table 1.1 (continued)

	All jobs	Low-skilled jobs
Life, physical, and social science	5.1	0.0
Legal	1.2	0.0
N	—	2,052

NOTE: Numbers represent the percentage in each category. N varies slightly with item-specific missing data. Data on the distribution of occupations are establishment data and are based on the number of occupations, not employment, within a firm, as is consistent with the BALS data.

SOURCE: Bay Area Longitudinal Surveys (BALS) Phone Survey (HIRE 2006) Bureau of Labor Statistics (2002a); U.S. Census Bureau (2003a).

(other than business services and education and medical services), trade (both retail and wholesale), and public administration all contain a disproportionately large number of low-skilled jobs.

Under the Occupation category, six types of jobs—office and administrative support, production, food preparation and serving, sales, building and grounds maintenance, and transportation and material moving—account for 84.5 percent of low-skilled jobs in the San Francisco Bay Area (results not shown) and 75.5 percent of low-skilled jobs nationwide, but only 34.6 percent of all positions nationwide. Office and administrative support account for over 40 percent of low-skilled positions but under 8 percent of all positions nationwide. Food preparation/serving and sales jobs each make up a little less than 10 percent of low-skilled positions but a little more than 2 percent of all positions nationwide.

Low-skilled jobs require relatively fewer skills than other jobs in many areas, which may explain their low educational and work experience requirements. Indeed, when we compare low-skilled jobs to other jobs in the U.S. economy, we see that the knowledge, skill, and ability requirements in low-skilled jobs are modest (Table 1.2). Low-skilled jobs have lower requirements in 21 of the 33 measures of knowledge, 27 of the 35 measures of skills, and 15 of the 51 measures of abilities.[2] The relatively lower requirements in low-skilled jobs all fall into areas that would be classified as new basic skills (academic, problem-solving, and communication skills).

Table 1.2 Knowledge, Skills, and Abilities Used in Low-Skilled Jobs

	All jobs	Low-skilled jobs
Knowledge		
Mechanical	52.0	60.0
Mathematics	74.1**	59.3
Skills		
Operation and control	66.6**	74.8
Equipment selection	78.7	71.9
Mathematics	80.0**	67.4
Reading comprehension	87.1**	66.7
Monitoring	83.4**	60.7
Active listening	75.9**	59.3
Writing	70.4**	57.0
Operation monitoring	50.3	53.3
Quality control analysis	70.7**	52.6
Equipment maintenance	40.6**	51.9
Speaking	71.2**	48.9
Low-skilled tasks		
Interact to accomplish a task		90.8
Exhibit appropriate behavior at work		85.3
Perceive cues from others		81.5
Read written instructions, safety warnings, labels, etc.		78.3
Write simple sentences, short notes, and simple memos		77.6
Fill out forms, record data, time		74.1
Read manuals, computer printouts, contracts, and agreements		73.8
Identify work-related problems		70.3
Prioritize tasks		68.8
Read forms, memos, and letters		67.6
Deal with customers		64.6
Use telephone systems		63.6
Problem-solve collaboratively		63.3
Gather information		62.6
Identify potential solutions to problems		52.9

Table 1.2 (continued)

	All jobs	Low-skilled jobs
Abilities		
Near vision	97.6**	91.1
Information ordering	94.1	89.6
Manual dexterity	69.6**	84.4
Problem sensitivity	88.9**	81.5
Wrist/finger speed	69.4**	80.7
Written comprehension	86.7**	76.3
Oral comprehension	81.9	75.6
Extent of flexibility	53.9**	74.8
Arm/hand steadiness	63.3**	74.1
Static strength	49.1**	74.1
Control precision	59.9**	70.4
Multilimb coordination	53.0**	70.4
Number facility	72.0	69.6
Trunk strength	56.5**	68.9
Finger dexterity	64.4	67.4
Selective attention	69.0	66.7
Oral expression	74.4**	61.5
Visualization	65.2	57.0
Written expression	68.7**	54.8
Deductive reasoning	82.3**	54.8
Time sharing	56.9	52.6
Perceptual speed	52.2	51.9
Reaction time	36.6**	51.9
Speed of limb movement	32.9**	51.1
Stamina	25.8**	51.1

NOTE: Information is only listed for skills required by at least half of the low-skilled jobs, defined as Job Zone 1 jobs. Data on knowledge, skills, and abilities (KSA) are from the O*NET database at www.onetcenter.org. A listing of all KSA in O*NET is available from the author. Numbers for knowledge, skills, and abilities represent the percentage of occupations that report that that particular knowledge, skill, or ability is important in the job. Importance is defined as a 3 or above on a 5-point scale in which 1 = not important and 5 = extremely important. ** indicates that significant ($p \leq 0.05$) differences exist between Job Zone 1 and all jobs, as determined by a t-test. Numbers for low-skilled tasks are from BALS data, described in Chapter 2, with information reported only for those tasks used in 50 percent or more of the BALS jobs. Numbers represent the percentage of jobs that report using the skill. Blank = not applicable.
SOURCE: Occupational Information Network (O*NET) Resource Center (USDOL 2006); Bay Area Longitudinal Surveys (BALS) data (HIRE 2006).

Despite the relatively low educational and work experience require-ments of low-skilled jobs, workers must use a relatively large number of skills on the job (Table 1.2). Most notably, physical and mechanical skills are required at higher levels in low-skilled jobs than in other jobs. Sixty percent of low-skilled jobs require mechanical knowledge, about 75 percent require operation and control skills, and over 80 percent require manual dexterity and wrist or finger speed. Physical abilities include manual dexterity, wrist/finger speed, extent of flexibility, arm/hand steadiness, static strength, control precision, multilimb coordina-tion, trunk strength, reaction time, speed of limb movement, and stam-ina.[3] Mechanical knowledge and skills include quality control analysis, operation and control, and equipment maintenance.

Most low-skilled jobs require workers to possess the new basics of academics (English and math), communication, and problem-solving. Communication skills are the most used: over 90 percent of low-skilled jobs require workers to interact with coworkers to accomplish a task, over 80 percent require workers to act appropriately at work and to per-ceive cues from others correctly, and over 60 percent require workers to deal with customers or work in teams. Academic skills also are heav-ily used in low-skilled jobs: over three-fourths require oral and written comprehension of English, including such skills as reading written in-structions, safety warnings, labels, invoices, work orders, logs, or jour-nals. Low-skilled workers are also required to write simple sentences, to fill out forms and logs, and to read manuals, computer printouts, con-tracts, agreements, forms, memos, and letters. Nearly 70 percent of the positions require workers to add and subtract. Over half of low-skilled jobs require oral and written expression. Workers in low-skilled posi-tions are also expected to problem-solve: over 54 percent of the posi-tions require deductive reasoning, and most of the jobs require workers to problem-solve, identify work-related problems, prioritize tasks, deal with customers, work in teams, or gather information.

WHO FILLS LOW-SKILLED POSITIONS?

Workers in low-skilled positions are often thought to be at the bot-tom of the workplace totem pole. They fill the positions that many of us held as youths or that we relegate to others for execution. Two distinct groups generally hold low-skilled jobs: youth and the economically disadvantaged. Youth, who by definition have little education or work experience, constitute as many as half of the workers in low-skilled jobs. Some youth are transitory participants in the low-skilled labor market, occupying those positions only until they complete their education or gain work skills on the job and advance beyond the entry-level, low-skilled positions. The other group, the economically disadvantaged, have a truncated education and intermittent work experience, and they frequently struggle in low-skilled employment throughout much of their life. For this group, low-skilled jobs are a way of life.

These two groups approach the labor market with vastly different expectations. Youth, especially youth that do not continue their education past high school, frequently flounder between jobs as they attempt to match their budding interests and skills with the appropriate job (Osterman 1980). In some cases, short-term youth joblessness (Becker and Hills 1980, 1983) and initial employment in minimum wage jobs (Carrington and Fallick 2001) eventually yield to long-term opportunities for advancement. In other cases, floundering creates long-term unemployment and harms career development because of a lack of work experience during the years of career formation, reducing subsequent wages (D'Amico and Maxwell 1994; Ellwood 1982; Lynch 1989; Meyer and Wise 1982). Youth that, for whatever reason, never fully integrate into the labor market and do not continue their education past high school can become mired in low-skilled jobs and enter the realm of the economically disadvantaged.

Both national and local databases make it easy to paint a statistical portrait of workers that potentially hold low-skilled jobs.[4] In 2000, about 44 percent of the U.S. population aged 25–64 could be considered to be in the labor market for low-skilled jobs, because these people had a high school education or less (U.S. Census Bureau 2003c). An additional 30 percent had some college, but, because these people did not have a college degree, they may have found themselves in low-skilled jobs. Individuals with only a high school education were disproportionately African American or from households in which English was not spoken (Table 1.3), and those disproportions increased in the older age groupings. In 1979, about 69 percent of a sample of youth aged 14–22 with a high school education or less were white, and about 78 percent

Table 1.3 Demographics and Cohort Aging of Workers in Low-Skilled Jobs (% of population)

| | U.S. population in 2000 (Age 25–64) | Age 14–22 in 1979 | High school education or less | | |
			Age 18–26 in 1983	Age 28–36 in 1993	Age 35–43 in 2000
Race					
White	76.3	69.3	68.0	60.9	60.6
Black	11.6	25.1	26.0	32.3	32.9
Other	12.1	5.6	6.0	6.8	6.5
N	1,472,037	12,610	8,545	5,281	4,512
Foreign language at home at age 14					
Yes	18.1	22.0	22.2	24.9	24.2
No	81.9	78.0	77.8	75.1	75.8
N	1,472,037	12,681	8,593	5,316	4,541

NOTE: 2000 U.S. population data are from the (weighted) 1 percent sample of the Public Use Microdata Samples (PUMS). Statistics in columns 2 through 5 are taken from the 1979 National Longitudinal Surveys and represent the percentage of the population in each category.
SOURCE: U.S. Census Bureau (2003c); Bureau of Labor Statistics (2002b).

spoke English in the home as an adolescent. Twenty-one years later, only 60.6 percent of members of the same group were white and 75.8 percent were from English-speaking families. This suggests that whites and individuals from English-speaking households have a greater tendency to continue their education beyond high school and, perhaps, move from low-skilled jobs at a more rapid rate than nonwhites and individuals from non-English-speaking households.

Individuals with only a high school education and little work experience—characteristics that roughly correspond to our definition of low-skilled job requirements—are more likely than individuals with more than a high school education and extensive work experience to have low wages and household income and to face labor market barriers (Table 1.4). Low-skilled individuals have hourly wages that are about half those of high-skilled individuals; such individuals are one-third as likely to receive tips or bonuses, and are four times as likely to live in a household with an income of less than $20,000.

The labor market challenges facing low-skilled individuals could prevent their becoming full participants in the labor market (Table 1.4). Potential challenges include youth (45 percent of low-skilled individuals are under 30, compared to only 20 percent of high-skilled individuals), greater child care responsibilities (over 80 percent of low-skilled individuals have children under 18), and less access to reliable transportation (low-skilled individuals are less likely to have a driver's license, insurance, regular access to a car, or own a car; and are more likely to use public transportation, walk, or use a friend or neighbor's car for their primary mode of transportation). Low-skilled individuals may be more likely to have health problems that inhibit them from working, as fewer are covered by health insurance and more of them have (or had) a substance abuse problem or a physical disability.

THE ECONOMIC ENVIRONMENT FACING WORKERS IN LOW-SKILLED POSITIONS

Throughout most of the twentieth century, the wage structure in the United States became more compressed (Goldin and Margo 1992). Although education levels were generally rising, a strong demand for

Table 1.4 Income and Labor Market Challenges for Workers with Low, Medium, and High Skill (% of population)

	Total	Low skill	Medium skill	High skill
Income				
Labor market				
Hourly rate of pay ($)	18.18	11.64	15.76**	20.78**
Tips or bonuses	27.1	22.6	18.9	33.2**
Household income				
Less than $20,000	16.1	31.9	17.4**	7.1**
$20,000–$49,999	33.8	23.7	37.7**	29.0
$50,000–$74,999	19.5	15.6	17.4	25.3**
$75,000–$99,999	11.2	6.7	12.6**	15.2**
$100,000–$249,999	7.4	2.2	4.9	13.4**
$250,000–$499,999	3.0	0.0	2.8**	5.2**
$500,000 or greater	0.4	0.0	0.4	0.7
Don't know	8.5	20.0	6.9**	4.1**
Labor market challenges				
Age				
18–25	16.3	31.9	23.0	7.9**
26–30	11.0	14.9	10.7	12.9
31–45	39.2	38.3	44.8	47.3
46–55	15.4	10.6	14.3	22.6**
56–64	7.7	1.4	4.0	8.6**
65 or older	10.3	2.8	3.2	0.7
Children				
Have children (under 18)	64.4	81.3	73.0	65.6**
Have children living in household	61.6	79.4	70.2**	61.6**
If yes, number of children	1.4	2.0	1.5**	1.3**
Taking care of children last week	40.1	56.7	42.1**	41.6**
Total number of children	1.5	2.2	1.7**	1.5**
Transportation				
Have valid driver's license	77.5	47.5	76.6**	93.5**
Have regular access to car	83.9	59.6	83.7**	96.4**
If yes, have car insurance	94.3	86.6	93.8**	97.0**
Typical mode of transportation				
Own car	79.2	50.4	78.6**	92.4**
Public	16.6	37.6	16.3**	7.6**
Walk	13.1	27.7	11.9**	6.5**
Friend or relative's car	6.7	14.9	5.6**	3.6**

Table 1.4 (continued)

	Total	Low skill	Medium skill	High skill
Medical				
Respondent covered by health insurance	81.7	62.9	76.6**	91.0**
Medical problem prevents employment	9.0	12.1	9.2	7.2
Mental health issues/depression	8.2	11.4	6.4	8.2
Substance abuse	6.6	11.3	5.6	5.0**
Physical abuse	6.8	10.6	6.0	5.7
Physical disability	7.8	12.3	8.3	5.7**
N	766	141	252	279

NOTE: Numbers represent the percentage of the population in each category. Total includes retired individuals. "Low skill" applies to individuals with only a high school education and no more than one year of work experience. "Medium skill" applies to individuals either having only a high school education *or* no more than one year of work experience. "High skill" applies to individuals with more than a high school education *and* more than one year of work experience. ** indicates a statistically significant ($p \leq 0.05$) difference, compared to low skill, as determined by a *t*-test.
SOURCE: Bay Area Longitudinal Surveys (BALS) Household Survey (HIRE 2006).

unskilled labor supported wages at the bottom end of the earnings distribution. Sometime during the 1970s this trend reversed, and by the late 1980s the wage dispersion was back to what it was in the 1950s. Workers at the bottom of the distribution began losing ground. Between 1963 and 1989, real average weekly wages for the least skilled workers declined by about five percent, while wages for the most skilled rose by about 40 percent (Juhn, Murphy, and Pierce 1993).[5]

The reasons for the increasing wage inequality are both varied and integrated; nonetheless, all agree that the economic changes underlying the growing gap have been great. Product market shifts from manufacturing to services (Murphy and Welch 1993) and the adding of skills to production and clerical jobs—traditional sources of employment for low-skilled workers (Cappelli 1993)—favored the more skilled workers in the labor market (Katz and Murphy 1992). These economic changes moved workers' jobs away from routine cognitive and manual tasks and toward nonroutine analytic and interactive tasks (Autor, Katz, and Krueger 1998; Autor, Levy, and Murnane 2003), which increased the demand for skills in our economy. As a consequence, skills became increasingly important in determining wages (Murnane, Willett, and Levy 1995), wage differentials (Teulings 1995), employment (Pryor and Schaffer 1999), and wage inequality (Juhn, Murphy, and Pierce 1993); and labor force participation declined among the less skilled (Juhn 1992). Declines in unionization (Freeman 1993) and in school quality (Card and Krueger 1992a), increases in competition (Revenga 1992) and in the use of technology (Autor, Katz, and Krueger 1998), and changes in federal policies (Sawicky 1999) also contributed to the shrinking economic opportunities for the low-skilled. As a result, individuals with below-average skills often remain unemployed or part of the working poor (Handel 2003), and they face increased spells and durations of nonemployment and job instability (Farber 1999) and higher job turnover (Holzer and LaLonde 2000) than more-skilled individuals.

The increased demand for skills also explains the deteriorating labor market for less-educated individuals (Autor, Katz, and Krueger 1998; Murnane, Willett, and Levy 1995), as the less-educated enter the labor market with few skills needed in the workplace (Card and Lemieux 2001). As a result, hiring has moved away from the less-educated and toward the more-educated (Murphy and Welch 1993), and the wage premium for college graduates has increased (Katz and Murphy 1992), which has decreased earnings (Levy and Murnane 1992) and employment (Murphy and Topel 1997; Juhn, Murphy, and Pierce 1993) among less-educated workers. Downturns in the business cycle have exacerbated the plight of less-skilled workers (Hoynes 2000), as college-educated or highly skilled individuals take jobs normally filled by high school–educated or lesser-skilled individuals (Devereux 2002).

THE ARGUMENT FOR SKILLS

These trends present a powerful argument for building skills in individuals with low levels of education to enhance their employment opportunities and wages. But which skills should be built? In a review of five studies on workforce readiness, the National Center for Research on Evaluation, Standards, and Student Testing identified three major categories of basic skills needed by lesser-skilled individuals in jobs:

academic skills, higher order thinking skills (problem-solving), and interpersonal and teamwork (communication) skills (O'Neil, Allred, and Baker 1997).[6] These basic skills—academic, problem-solving, and communication skills—frequently serve as a foundation for vocational skills used in the workplace. In fact, policies and programs designed to make individuals workforce-ready (e.g., the Workforce Investment Act, Welfare-to-Work, School-to-Work) begin by building these basic skills and, if the individual is still not employed, continue training to provide more specific workplace skills.

Research also supports the need for building a strong foundation in these basic skills. Academic skills increase employment (Johnson and Corcoran 2003) and job stability (Holzer and LaLonde 2000) for low-wage workers and determine their wages (Murnane, Willett, and Levy 1995), most probably because employers of low-wage workers require these skills. Over half of the employers in the Multi-City Study of Urban Inequality required daily reading of at least a paragraph, about half required the use of computers and arithmetic, and nearly half required writing—all academic skills. These same employers also value basic communication skills, particularly in retail firms (Moss and Tilly 2001). Specific workplace skills, which are often acquired on the job, were required by under half of the low-wage Multi-City employers (Holzer 1996). The only specific workplace skill required by at least half of the employers was computers (Autor, Katz, and Krueger 1998; Bartel and Lichtenberg 1987), which some consider to be the fifth component of the new basic skills (Murnane and Levy 1996).

POLICY SOLUTIONS

Suggestions abound as to what policies might be implemented to ensure access to Horatio Alger–type success for individuals, and many of the policy proposals are grounded in a philosophy of how the economy best functions. Free market advocates favor no policy interventions, believing that market-produced incentives will lead individuals to invest in the skills that improve their economic opportunities. A more collectivist approach, one frequently taken by unions and grassroots community organizations, favors policies that limit market-produced incentives by mandating outcomes. Public service employment, restrictions on immigration and trade to limit the supply of workers, and policies to raise wages (e.g., minimum and living wages or wage supports) and employer-funded benefits may be considered examples. A collectivist philosophy underlies many of the publicly funded safety nets and programs that provide support to low-income individuals as they gain necessary labor market skills. Support can be economic (e.g., income supplements), social (child care, gang prevention), or psychological (drug abuse counseling).

Arguably, most policies fall somewhere between the free market and the collectivist perspective by proposing modest interventions in a market-driven economy. Such policies use incentives or capacity building so that either firms or individuals become fully engaged participants in a relatively free market economy. Some such interventionist policies focus on the supply side of the labor market and build human capital. Most prominent among such efforts are two types: 1) public education—an individual's "first chance" for building skills using public dollars—and 2) publicly provided training programs—a "second chance" for individuals that fail to get the requisite skills through education.

Other interventionist policies focus on the demand side of the labor market and stimulate employers' demand for labor. The general tenet of labor demand policies is that jobs are in short supply. Even when unemployment is low, many groups—those with less education, racial minorities, and residents in high unemployment areas—have difficulty finding a job. In this vein, policies that stimulate the economy and expand the number of jobs, while still monitoring levels of inflation, benefit everyone, including groups that face employment difficulties. "A rising tide lifts all boats" aptly describes the philosophy underlying this approach.

Of course, few programs fit neatly into only one of these classifications—in part because policy goals are often multipurposed and overlapping. Still, the categorization provides a useful way to structure discussions about policies designed to facilitate more efficient and equitable labor market outcomes for workers in low-skilled jobs.

FIRST CHANCE: BUILDING SKILLS IN PUBLIC SCHOOLS

Providing public school students with the knowledge and skills needed in the labor market was at the heart of the School-to-Work Opportunities Act (STWOA) of 1994, which was designed to address the employment problems of youth leaving high school, whether as graduates or dropouts. Concern about the basic skills of our youth began at least a decade earlier, when *A Nation at Risk* took schools to task for their mediocre performance in building students' academic skills (National Commission on Excellence in Education 1983). The continued decline in student performance after the tempest caused by *A Nation at Risk* prompted educators to launch the Back-to-Basics programs of the 1980s, and the continued employment problems of the largely forgotten half of youth that do not graduate from college led to a new vision for secondary education: integrate academic and workplace skills into the curriculum to motivate learning and increase skills in American youth. Two pieces of federal legislation addressed this integration. The Carl D. Perkins Vocational and Technical Education Act of 1998 (Perkins III) integrated academic skills into traditional vocational education, and STWOA integrated workplace skill-building into academic programs.

Both pieces of legislation sought to ease youths' transition from school to work by increasing their academic and workplace skills. If school-to-work programs could build both the academic and the workplace skills needed in the local labor market, the half of youth not graduating from college could transition into well-paying, stable careers (Bernhardt et al. 2001; Halperin 1998). Programs in European secondary schools have had apparent success at easing youth's transition into the labor market by instilling in students job skills that connect with local employers' needs (Vickers 1995). This suggests that a successful school-to-work program could increase employability among youth if it developed skills needed by local employers.

The success of school-to-work programs rests on the assumption that building skills that are in demand in the local labor market will increase employment and wages for those youth whose formal education ends with high school. Research has shown modest employment and wage gains for program participants (Kemple 2001), and yet the school-to-work legislation was not reauthorized. What went wrong?

One possibility was that STWOA did not hold schools accountable for poor performance and that educational decision-making moved away from states and communities, which had the best knowledge of student needs. In 2001, No Child Left Behind shifted federal funds toward increasing the accountability of schools to produce results, giving more freedom to states and communities in using federal education funds, rewarding proven educational methods, and providing more choices for parents. Gone was STWOA's emphasis of linking skill-building in schools to the needs of the local labor market.

Educational policies that change the nature of public education and its incentives can have far-reaching effects. In Fall 2003, public schools served about 85.7 percent of the nation's students, including about 48 million elementary and secondary students (Snyder, Tan, and Hoffman 2004). The predominance of enrollment in public schools means that federal policies that alter the educational environment have an impact on the entirety of the nation's education, public and private.

SECOND CHANCE: OUT-OF-SCHOOL PROGRAMS

Arguably, one of the policies most often targeted at building labor market skills is that of publicly funded employment and training programs. (LaLonde [1995] provides a history of such programs; D'Amico [2005] provides an assessment.) If public expenditures on employment and training programs increase skills through program participation or improved labor market information and employment matches, such investments can prove beneficial to all involved. Participants gain either productive skills or information that leads to employment and increased earnings. Government comes out ahead, too, because participants reduce their dependence on social welfare benefits and increase their tax payments through their increased earnings. And employers gain productive workers.

Current attempts to build such a second-chance system are grounded in the 1998 Workforce Investment Act (WIA). WIA folded earlier training dollars into a universal system of employment and training services for all youth, unemployed persons, and incumbent workers by mandating the development of One-Stop Career Centers in every community. The goal of One-Stops is to provide high-quality job train-ing, employment, labor market information, and income maintenance services using WIA dollars to fund employment and training activities as well as activities connecting participants to other job- and education-related services. Critical to WIA funding is the discretionary ability of local areas to tailor training dollars to the specific needs of local busi-nesses and potential workers. Most WIA training dollars, like the Tem-porary Aid to Needy Families (TANF) training dollars discussed below, are for short-term (six months or less) training.

WIA's second-chance programs provide a relatively high volume of services. WIA's One Stop services served about eight million individu-als from January 1 to March 31, 2005, and served an additional 300,000 young people in its programs for youth during that time (USDOL 2005). About 7.8 million individuals accessed WIA's Employment Services during the first three months of 2005, and about 300,000 dislocated workers and 387,000 adults in total participated in work activities or received job training.

DEMAND SIDE

Debate exists about how well macroeconomic stimulants increase employment rates, wages, and occupational upgrading for the low-skilled. Some believe that policies to reduce capital gain taxes in order to spur business investment and growth, along with policies to cut per-sonal tax in order to increase take-home pay and demand, benefit pri-marily the middle- and upper-tiered earners (Danziger and Gottschalk 1986). Still, targeted labor demand policies, in which stimulants are structured to increase employment and earnings for low-income work-ers (e.g., the Earned Income Tax Credit), can disproportionately benefit low-wage workers (Bartik 2001).

Some advocates of demand-side policies find fault with the pay-ments made to low-wage workers and propose a living wage that would elevate workers' pay enough to allow them to rise out of poverty, despite the potential of such measures to reduce employment opportunities for these workers (Fairris and Reich [2005] and other articles in the same issue of *Industrial Relations*). Other advocates have somewhat more collectivist goals and argue that more direct interventions in a firm's employment practices are needed. They propose wage subsidies, profit-sharing, public employment, and workplace governance actions such as antidiscrimination restrictions to increase employment of low-skilled individuals, presumably without shifting employment from one group to another or stimulating inflation (Freeman and Gottschalk 1998). Program advocates of demand-side policies often argue that such policies are most effective when combined with support services that encourage job retention and build economic and psychological self-sufficiency (Kazis and Miller 2001). However, most targeted labor demand policies have been experimental at best and have not seen widespread implementation (Bartik 2001).

SAFETY NETS

The Personal Responsibility and Work Opportunity Reconciliation Act (PRWORA) of 1996 represented the most radical reform of general income support to low-income families since the expansion of such programs in the 1930s. PRWORA fundamentally changed the nature of welfare funding, placed limits on the amount of time welfare could be received, and created work requirements for recipients receiving TANF.[7]

These legislative changes reflected a philosophical shift in view toward low-income (which are frequently low-skilled) individuals. No longer were they entitled to a lifetime safety net should their labor market efforts bring low earnings. Instead they could receive temporary assistance while striving to gain employment at higher-paying jobs.[8] To help them achieve economic self-sufficiency through labor market earnings, the government requires most TANF recipients to participate in work activities.[9] No more than 20 percent of recipients can participate in vocational training (generally defined as longer-term training of more than six months in duration) for the work activity. TANF programs are viewed as successful at moving individuals into the labor market but as not always successful at placing individuals in jobs with wages leading to economic self-sufficiency (Hamilton et al. 2001).

SUMMARY

Economic outcomes for workers with relatively few skills have worsened in the past few decades as the demand for skills in the labor market has increased. In response to these changes, policies increasingly have emphasized skill-building and employability within a local labor market as a way to improve the labor market outcomes of low-skilled individuals. Data presented in this chapter suggest that this emphasis is warranted. So-called low-skilled jobs are not no-skilled jobs. Workers in low-skilled jobs are required to possess a wide variety of skills for those jobs' successful execution. Although low-skilled jobs require relatively fewer skills than other jobs, the preponderance of data presented in this chapter suggests that low-skilled jobs require a fair number of skills. Low-skilled jobs require workers to use new basic skills (English, math, problem-solving, and communication) and require them to behave appropriately and to correctly perceive cues from others. And low-skilled jobs require physical and mechanical skills at higher levels than other jobs.

Given the centrality of skills in accomplishing even low-skilled jobs, it is somewhat surprising that research has not put skills at the focal point in describing the labor market for workers in low-skilled jobs. Although research has linked the general increase in demand for skilled labor to economic outcomes for workers with high skills (Cawley et al. 2000; Blackburn and Neumark 1993), it has not made the link for workers in low-skilled positions, in part because data limitations have precluded such analyses.

This study shifts the focus toward skills when studying the labor market for workers in low-skilled jobs. We use information from a single California labor market—the San Francisco Bay Area—to highlight the knowledge and skills that employers require in low-skilled jobs and those that individuals supply. By showing the centrality of skills in low-skilled jobs, we show how firms structure recruiting, hiring, compensation, and promotion opportunities in entry-level, low-skilled jobs. In other words, we show how (and why) the demand for skills in low-skilled jobs structures the work life for workers in such jobs.

Notes

1. We use the U.S. Department of Labor's (USDOL) Occupational Information Network (O*NET) database (USDOL 2006) to describe the knowledges, skills, and attitudes needed to perform a wide variety of jobs throughout the economy. We use the Bay Area Longitudinal Surveys (BALS), detailed in Chapter 2, to describe specific tasks of low-skilled jobs.

2. Table 1.2 does not present the complete list of O*NET's knowledges, skills, and abilities. It presents only those that are used in 50 percent or more of Job Zone 1 jobs.

3. Because Table 1.2 lists only knowledges, skills, and abilities required in 50 percent or more of low-skilled jobs, some physical and mechanical skills are left out. Among the physical abilities not listed are dynamic strength, spatial orientation, dynamic flexibility, response orientation, explosive strength, and overall body coordination.

4. We use the Census Public Use Microdata Sample [PUMS] (U.S. Census Bureau 2003c) to describe a cross-section of the population aged 25–64 in 2000 with no more than a high school education; we use the National Longitudinal Surveys youth sample [NLSY79] (BLS 2002b) to describe how the composition of individuals with no more than a high school degree changes as it ages; and we use the Bay Area Longitudinal Surveys [BALS] (HIRE 2006), discussed in Chapter 2, to describe the characteristics of and challenges facing low-skilled individuals as compared to individuals with higher levels of skills.

5. The growing gap between economic outcomes for the haves and the have-nots is impervious to the definition of have-nots. "Have-nots" can be defined as individuals with low levels of education (Blackburn, Bloom, and Freeman 1990), individuals with low skills (Autor, Levy, and Murnane 2003), children in poverty (Iceland et al. 2001), or members of racial or ethnic minorities (Bound and Holzer 1993). Definitions of economic outcomes also seem not to matter. Earnings (Levy and Murnane 1992), employment (Murphy and Topel 1997; Juhn 1992), wealth (Levy and Michel 1991), and income (Levy 1987) eroded for the have-nots, while the wage premium for education for high-ability workers (Cawley et al. 2000; Blackburn and Neumark 1993) and inequality (Karoly 1993) increased.

6. A fourth category exists in the framework that is not skill-based: personal characteristics and attitudes.

7. Funding changed from income support to families with children (Aid to Families with Dependent Children, or AFDC)—including separate programs for employment and training (Job Opportunity and Basic Skills, or JOBS) and assistance (Emergency Assistance, or EA)—to money from block grants to states for a single, capped entitlement.

8. Recipients under the old legislation remained eligible for benefits as long as they met program eligibility rules. Under PRWORA, federally funded welfare assistance exists only for five cumulative years (60 months). States can exempt up to

20 percent of their caseload from this time limit by using state funds to provide assistance to families beyond the federal time limit.

9. Prior to PRWORA, states were required to offer basic work activities to recipients (e.g., basic and secondary education; English as a Second Language programs; job skills training; and job development, placement, and readiness) and at least two of the less basic activities (e.g., job search, on-the-job training, work supplements, or community work experience) as a part of the old training program (JOBS).

2
Local Labor Markets and Low-Skilled Jobs

Theory and Data

My long-term goal is to graduate. A longer-term goal is to become a lawyer. There is a little phrase I use and some people don't like it but it goes like this: "I want to learn how to screw the system before the system screws me." I don't mean it in a bad way; it is just the fact that I want to learn how to manage the system, because I know it is difficult to understand the laws. My family and [other] people have been screwed over and for the simple fact of being ignorant. But they just don't know.
—A low-income adult

Characterizing labor markets for workers in low-skilled jobs is, on the one hand, easy. If employers view jobs as not requiring skills to perform, workers in such positions become a homogeneous commodity, and a competitive market for their services develops. Market forces (e.g., business and product cycles, supply of available workers) will determine workers' wages and probability of employment (Bulow and Summers 1986; Weiss 1980). The seemingly inexhaustible supply of workers, all of whom can successfully perform in the job, leaves firms with little incentive to provide workers in low-skilled positions with job security or the ability to move beyond the entry-level, low-skilled job.

On the other hand, the market for workers in low-skilled positions may be complex. If employers view low-skilled jobs as requiring skills, workers in such positions can be differentiated and a market for their skills will develop. Individuals with skills in relatively short supply in the labor market will garner increased wages as employers compete for their skills by bidding on their services. Profit-maximizing firms will develop long-term strategies for retaining workers with needed skills, since recruiting and turnover costs make their replacement costly. As a result of these actions, workers with needed skills will have above-market wages (Akerlof and Yellen 1986; Weiss 1990), protection from layoffs and economic downturns (Rebitzer and Taylor 1991), and career progression potential (Keane and Wolpin 1997) through opportunities for promotion (Baker, Gibbs, and Holmstrom 1994; McCue 1996).

This chapter develops a conventional description of the market for workers in low-skilled jobs and an alternative to it. The conventional model is grounded in a competitive market for the services of workers in low-skilled jobs, and the alternative is grounded in a market for their skills. We also describe the data used to determine whether the conventional model aptly depicts the market for workers in low-skilled positions. The data, which come from a local labor market in California, allow us to ferret out the actions taken by employers in recruiting, hiring, compensating, and retaining workers in low-skilled positions and to assess the consistency of these actions with the conventional model. Ultimately, it is our comparison of firms' behavior to the conventional description that illustrates how labor markets for workers in low-skilled jobs operate.

THE CONVENTIONAL DESCRIPTION OF THE MARKET FOR WORKERS IN LOW-SKILLED JOBS

The notion that competitive labor markets set wages and employment for workers in low-skilled jobs was formalized in the late 1960s and early 1970s as part of the dual labor market theory.[1] Dual labor market theorists maintained that jobs can be divided into two groups. The secondary labor market contains jobs characterized by low wages, bad working conditions, unstable employment, and little opportunity for advancement. The primary labor market contains jobs with high wages, good working conditions, and opportunities for advancement into higher-paying jobs (Doeringer and Piore 1971). While the dual labor market theory initially was contrasted with human capital theory as a framework for explaining employment and wages (Leigh 1976; Piore 1983; Woodbury 1979), more recent views of labor market operations have integrated the two theories (Dickens and Lang 1992; Lang and Dickens 1988) as human capital theory has incorporated an endogeneity of above-market wages paid to skilled workers and wage rigidities created by social institutions (Akcrlof 1980).

The integration of theories at the microlevel helps explain persistent unemployment for unskilled workers (Saint-Paul 1997), as above-market wages paid to skilled workers limit access to the primary labor market jobs and cause markets not to clear. As the excess supply of workers moves from the primary into the secondary labor market, unemployment rises among less-skilled workers and their wages fall. These processes are not contingent on the existence of two distinct labor markets but can arise in a continuum of skill levels. If more-skilled workers receive above-market wages, an excess supply of workers at each of the higher skill levels develops. As the excess supply of workers at one skill level develops, workers bump down into the next skill level of positions, leaving unemployment among the least skilled workers.[2]

The oversupply of workers in low-skilled jobs leaves incumbents with low wages and little job security. Because the skills required in low-skilled jobs are ubiquitous (or, by another way of thinking, nonexistent), firms view workers as homogeneous and behave as if the supply of labor is perfectly elastic at relatively low wages. Firms face few turnover costs from worker separations and provide few incentives for workers to remain with the firm (e.g., little chance for upward mobility). This conventional description of the labor market for workers in low-skilled jobs provides a benchmark against which to examine its actual operation.

AN ALTERNATIVE TO THE CONVENTIONAL VIEW

The conventional description of the labor market for workers in low-skilled jobs seems to be at odds with recent studies describing employment for low-wage workers (and with the data presented in Chapter 1), which hint at the possibility that workers in low-skilled jobs have skills. Workers' considerable mobility in passing into and out of low-earning employment (Holzer, Lane, and Vilhuber 2004) suggests that some workers in low-skilled jobs possess the skills needed in better-paying and higher-skilled jobs. The positive wage gains from job turnover among less-skilled workers (Gladden and Taber 2000; Royalty

1998) suggest that career paths or promotion opportunities can develop in low-skilled jobs. Still other research shows that work experience (Burtless 1995) and cognitive skills (Holzer and LaLonde 2000; Tyler, Murnane, and Willett 2000) provide a return for low-wage workers, suggesting that firms value skills held by workers in low-skilled jobs.

Such research highlights a potential heterogeneity among workers in low-skilled jobs—a proposition that would make the hiring process more costly as firms search for workers with the skills needed for the job. It matters not if the skills needed are skills of a relatively low level; it matters only that turnover and hiring costs accrue with worker separations. Of course, turnover and search costs increase with the skill requirements of the job, especially if the skills are job-specific or in relatively short supply, but even modest costs will provide incentives for firms to develop strategies for recruiting, hiring, and retaining workers with needed skills.

Turnover costs create efficiency incentives for profit-maximizing firms to pay above-market wages for skills, as such wages increase the cost of separation for workers (Salop 1979). The incentives provided by above-market wages also allow a firm to do three things: 1) decrease hiring costs, which occur because information about an applicant's skills and work effort are unknown (Bowles 1985; Bulow and Summers 1986; Shapiro and Stiglitz 1984; Weiss 1980); 2) eliminate the moral hazard of employee dishonesty (Stoft 1982); and 3) improve workers' morale (Shapiro and Stiglitz 1984).

If firms need skills, they will increase wages for workers who possess skills that are in relatively short supply. The fact that these workers are relatively less skilled than workers in more highly skilled jobs should not matter as much as the need for firms to increase wages to attract the skills they have a demand for. Even if firms require such seemingly basic skills as honesty, reliability, and integrity, if not enough workers possess these skills to meet the needs of all firms, firms will engage in rather lengthy and expensive recruiting and screening processes to obtain honest workers. It follows that firms might raise wages to recruit and retain honest workers, and might even develop incentives for them to stay on the job once hired. The market for skills of workers in low-skilled positions presents an alternative to our conventional model. Our study of the operation of a local labor market will provide evidence as to which is the more appropriate description—the conventional or the alternative.

OUR DATA

Analyzing the dynamics of a local labor market increases our understanding of the market for workers in low-skilled jobs by highlighting the interplay between skills, firm behavior, and wages in such jobs. We examine this interplay by overlaying on this local market four conceptual aspects of the conventional model of the labor market for workers in low-skilled positions: 1) skill requirements, 2) wage determination, 3) recruiting and screening behavior, and 4) promotion opportunities. The actual operation of the market will determine the relative makeup of these four parts. In relation to these four concepts, firms can take four actions: 1) require heterogeneous skills in low-skilled jobs, 2) increase wages when skills are in relatively short supply, 3) structure recruiting methods to attract workers who possess the skills needed in low-skilled positions, and 4) provide advancement opportunities from entry-level, low-skilled positions. If firms do these things, evidence suggests that the labor market for workers in low-skilled positions will be a market for skills and not the competitive market described in our conventional model.

Such an examination requires a unique database, as analysis must be grounded in firm-level data that yields the following: a detailed description of the skills needed in low-skilled positions; information on a firm's recruiting and hiring behavior, compensation, and internal labor market structure; and information on the market forces affecting the firm's decision-making about workers in low-skilled positions. The Bay Area Longitudinal Surveys (BALS), drawn from three counties in the San Francisco Bay Area, provide such information, and this book uses them to describe how a local labor market allocates workers to low-skilled jobs.[3] Of course, like any local labor market, the labor market depicted in BALS contains idiosyncrasies that might color its operation. It is therefore important to understand local conditions that might differentiate the BALS labor market from other labor markets for workers in low-skilled positions.

The BALS Local Labor Market

The popular view of California in decades past evoked images of growth, prosperity, sun, and surf. California of late conjures images of high housing prices, economic difficulties, and political crises. In reality, California includes both sets of images. California holds 12.2 percent of the nation's population and 30.8 percent of the nation's Hispanic or Latino population (39.8 percent of the Mexican-origin population).[4] Housing is at a premium, as homeowner and rental vacancy rates are well below the national average and the percentage of owner-occupied housing is nearly 10 percentage points below the national average.[5] California households contain an average of one-third of a person more than do the nation's households (U.S. Census Bureau 2003b).

Within California, the San Francisco Bay Area serves as a magnet for people of all types seeking work. In 2002, the 11-county San Jose–San Francisco–Oakland Combined Statistical Area (CSA) contained more than seven million individuals, but no demographic group made up a majority, although 49 percent of the population was white and non-Hispanic. The Bay Area attracts a highly educated population: over 86 percent of the population that was 25 and older in 2002 had graduated from high school, and 40 percent held at least a bachelor's degree. San Francisco County had the eighth highest percentage in the nation of residents holding a bachelor's degree or higher (45 percent). Given the plethora of highly educated individuals in the Bay Area, it is not surprising that 44 percent of the population works as managers or professionals, compared with 34 percent nationwide (U.S. Census Bureau 2003b).

The Bay Area's attractiveness also makes it a magnet for people from other countries. In 2002, nearly 30 percent of its population was foreign-born, and three Bay Area counties were in the top 10 counties in the nation in percentage of foreign-born population. Extremely high housing costs often are viewed as the price one pays for living in the Bay Area. The area contained eight of the 10 counties in the nation with the highest-valued median housing units (owner-occupied). Rental prices were also high, as five of the 10 counties with the highest median monthly housing costs for renter-occupied units were located in the Bay Area (U.S. Census Bureau 2003b).

As this description might suggest, some individuals look at California and the Bay Area and see unusual or just plain odd demographics. Others, however, see it as the bellwether for the nation. National leaders often look toward California to anticipate trends. California led the nation into the information technology age, and its demographic diversity challenged other states to examine their bilingual education policies. In this vein, California labor markets serve as a barometer for labor markets across the nation. Their ability to integrate workers whose second (or third) language is English into the labor market, to provide a living wage to workers struggling in a high-cost environment, and to weather large fluctuations in economic activity (like the birth and death of dot-com firms) serves as an indicator for a nation struggling with these emerging issues.

The BALS Data

As a local labor market grappling with the emerging trends facing firms with low-skilled jobs—immigration, language barriers, escalating housing prices, and the need for highly educated workers—the Bay Area provides a near-ideal laboratory in which to examine the labor market for workers in low-skilled jobs. Fortunately, the Bay Area Longitudinal Surveys (BALS) data provide an opportunity to use the area for such an examination.

The BALS research project randomly selected firms in three counties of the San Francisco Bay Area (Alameda, San Francisco, and San Joaquin) to survey about the knowledge and skill requirements and employment conditions of their low-skilled positions, defined as those requiring no more than a high school education and one year of work experience. Comparable surveys were administered to households in a low-income Alameda County community to obtain information about the skills held by individuals residing in the BALS labor market.[6]

The three-county BALS area could be considered a microcosm of many urban areas in the country.[7] San Francisco County is a highly dense urban center that has transitioned into a white collar–based "new economy." Employment in professional services and growth in the high-tech sector created fortunes for many but left others with minimal employment opportunities and an inability to sustain themselves in a city with escalating land and housing prices. Across the bay, Alameda County caught the overflow from the area's dot-com boom. Rising rents in San Francisco, to the county's west, and Silicon Valley, to its south, sent businesses and individuals scurrying to the relatively more affordable Alameda County. There, a more traditional manufacturing/health care/trade-based economy welcomed the new arrivals, who were still within commuting distance of San Francisco and Silicon Valley (EDAB 2001). Continued escalating prices sent businesses and individuals farther west into the Stockton-Lodi MSA in San Joaquin County (Zito 2003). Even though its location—it shares a border with Alameda County and is in relative proximity to Silicon Valley—has opened the floodgates to commuters and businesses wanting refuge from the inner Bay Area counties, this Central Valley county maintains a rural texture, having 808,838 acres of farmland and only 402.9 persons per square mile. Although in 2000 about one-third of San Joaquin County was Hispanic (many of the Hispanics are migrant farm workers), it was the only county of the three with a demographic majority, that being white.

BALS administered surveys to employers in this three-county area in two waves from June 1998 through December 2003.[8] The rapid deterioration of the Bay Area labor market, starting in early 2001 and continuing through most of the surveying, provided a natural experiment of sorts for identifying market influences on low-skilled positions.

Wave I BALS surveying was designed to obtain critical information from human resource managers and line supervisors about the knowledge and skills necessary for individuals to obtain, retain, succeed in, and advance from entry-level, low-skilled jobs, and on the outcomes associated with employment in low-skilled positions. This information was gathered in a two-stage process. Initially, 5,514 randomly selected firms were called (the Phone Survey) to gain cursory information about the firm and its low-skilled positions, identify firms with such positions available, and solicit participation for a more in-depth, on-site survey. Some 405 of the firms hiring in low-skilled positions participated in this on-site, in-depth survey to collect information about one specific position (the Employer Survey).[9] The Employer Survey was designed to obtain information from human resource managers on recruiting, screening, and employing workers in an entry-level, low-skilled position and to obtain information from line supervisors on the knowledge and skills necessary to succeed in and advance from that position.[10] Wave I surveying was conducted from June 1998 through October 2002.

In Wave II, the 405 firms participating in the Wave I Employer Survey were resurveyed anywhere from 12 to 56 months after their initial surveying (an average of 22.8 months passed between surveys) to determine changes over time in job requirements, characteristics, and compensation (the Longitudinal Survey). Wave II surveys were administered from October 2002 through December 2003.

Random selection of firms in Wave I surveying was stratified by county and number of employees in the firm to ensure meaningful analysis along these lines.[11] Within each of the three counties, BALS targeted the Employer Survey at three sizes of firms: small (1–49 employees), medium (100–249 employees), and large (over 300 employees).[12] There are gaps between the size categories to create a distinct difference between a small and a medium or a medium and a large firm. Otherwise, firms of different sizes might differ by only one employee.

Wave 1 surveying began in the summer of 1998 with large firms in San Francisco County. From June 1999 to February 2000, BALS surveying expanded in San Francisco County to include 25 surveys in each firm size.[13] In December 2000, the geographic scope of BALS increased to include Alameda County, an effort that consumed nearly 11 months and that also included two months of summer surveying in San Joaquin County. In all, 327 firms were surveyed during this period, a time in which the Bay Area labor market was relatively tight.[14] Soon thereafter the dot-com bust sent unemployment skyrocketing, creating a vastly different labor market. To capture potential differences in firms' behavior in tight and loose labor markets through cross-sectional analysis, BALS reentered the field in Alameda County during Summer 2002, when the unemployment rate stood at 7.0 percent, to administer the Employer Survey to 78 firms. The BALS Longitudinal Survey, administered from October 2002 through December 2003, also affords a comparison of tight and loose labor markets.[15] Because unemployment rates exceeded 6.0 percent during most of the longitudinal surveying, most firms moved from a tight to a loose labor market between the two survey periods.

In 2002, BALS expanded its surveying efforts to include households in one zip code of Alameda County.[16] The Household Survey collected information from individuals about their job skills, social service needs, and employment characteristics.[17] The community in which the survey was conducted, often described as working class, is an ideal setting for obtaining information on the skills held by individuals who might be hired for low-skilled positions. The community's location in the heart of the Bay Area means that employers in the three-county BALS area rely heavily on its population for workers. Twenty-five percent of all workers in the BALS counties reside in the zip code's county, and 63.9 percent of the workers living in the county work in the BALS local labor market.[18] The Household Survey was administered face-to-face to 766 individuals, including a random sampling of 675 households and 91 individuals using social service agencies in the community, and was designed to collect from individuals information that was parallel to that obtained from firms in the Employer Survey.

Skills in the BALS Labor Market

The BALS Employer Survey asked employers whether jobs required workers in the low-skilled positions to perform tasks using certain skills. There were 53 skills in all, which were grouped into six areas: reading and writing in English (8 specific skills), math (9 specific skills), communication (8 specific skills), problem-solving (11 specific skills), use of equipment (7 specific skills), and use of computer software (10 specific skills).[19] Each specific skill (and each grouping) was included in data collection because employers had described the use of that skill or grouping in low-skilled positions in focus group discussions. These skills were translated into survey language for individuals through a series of informal focus groups containing individuals from the population under study.

One might expect to find a complementarity in skills used in the low-skilled job selected for study, such that positions requiring one skill might also require another. In such cases, identifiable sets of skills will be required in a specific low-skilled position, no matter who the employer is. For example, jobs requiring physical strength might also require large motor skills and English communication skills. A strong worker might be adept at lifting heavy packages, but he is of little use without the coordination to place them where needed with contents unbroken and the ability to read package labels, complete tracking forms, and tell other haulers that he has completed the task. Such sets of skills as this would be used consistently by all employers.

We identified skill sets in low-skilled jobs using a factor analysis on each of the six skill groupings. The factor analysis identified 15 unique skill sets in low-skilled jobs, using the correlations of individual skills to uncover patterns in each skill grouping. These patterns, called factors, were developed into skill sets using the most highly correlated skills in each factor.[20] Specifically, we measured the intensity of skill use in each low-skilled job by computing a factor score from the loadings (i.e., correlations) on each factor.[21] Because the factor score uses a z-score scale that ranges from approximately −3.0 to +3.0, it provides a weighted measure of how much each skill set is used in a job.

Our factor analysis identified two distinct types of skill sets used in low-skilled positions in the BALS local labor market. Our measure of the first type, new basic skills, corresponds closely with the skills uncovered by Murnane and Levy (1996) using case studies of management practices at Diamond Star Motors, Northwestern Mutual, and Honda. This research shows that jobs for low-wage workers require both the general skills of punctuality, hard work, and a positive attitude and the "new basic skills" of reading, math, problem-solving, communication, and computers. Our measure of the second type of skill set from the BALS labor market, job equipment skills, reflects what might be considered more traditional blue- and pink-collar skills used in low-skilled positions.

Our new basic skill sets include two types of reading and writing in English skills (simple and complex), three types of math skills (algebra, applied math, and measurement), three types of problem-solving skills (prioritizing, evaluating, and leading), two types of communication skills (working with customers and with coworkers), and three types of computer software skills (productivity enhancers, multimedia, and financial). Our job equipment skill sets include two types of equipment usage: office and production.

Table 2.1 links specific skills to each of the skill sets and compares supply and demand for each of these skills. The first column shows the percentage of employers who say they need a certain skill in an entry-level, low-skilled job; the second, third, and fourth columns list the percentage of workers of various levels of skill who feel confident they can supply that skill. For instance, whereas 70.3 percent of employers want an employee who can spot work-related problems (a skill in the

Table 2.1 Demand for and Supply of Skills in the BALS Labor Market

New basic skills	Demand (% employers needing)	Supply (% employees who say they have)		
		Low- and mid-skilled	Low-skilled	All
English skill sets				
Simple English				
Read written instructions	78.3[a]	66.2**	55.3***	76.6
Read forms, memos, and letters	67.6	66.7	57.4***	76.8***
Read manuals, computer printouts, contracts, and agreements	73.8[a]	46.8**	42.6***	57.6***
Write simple sentences, short notes, and simple memos	77.6[a]	35.2**	42.6***	65.8***
Fill out forms, record data or time into log or chart	74.1[a]	44.8**	31.9***	60.1**
Complex English				
Write letters using correct structure and sentence style	24.2	34.1[a]**	23.2	48.8**
Proofread	23.4	38.7[a]***	31.2***	50.9***
Organize information into a brief written report	22.9	28.2	19.1	41.8**
Math skill sets				
Algebra				
Use ratios, fractions, decimals, or percentages	27.4	32.8	27.0	44.2**
Estimate or round off numbers	32.7	51.1[a]***	39.7	65.3***
Solve simple equations	34.2	41.7[a]***	27.0	51.8***
Interpret data from graphs, tables, or charts	13.5	33.6[a]***	22.7**	47.5***
Applied				
Make change	30.7	81.7[a]***	75.2***	87.5***
Compute or figure discounts, markups, or selling price	17.2	47.3[a]***	39.7**	58.9***

37

Use equipment such as a calculator, cash register, or business machine	43.9	64.4[a]**	50.4	74.3**
Measurement				
Perform simple measurements (e.g., lengths, volumes)	41.6	67.2[a]***	58.2**	74.1**
Use measurement instruments (e.g., ruler, scale)	44.9	67.9[a]***	55.3**	74.4**
Problem-solving skill sets				
Prioritization				
Prioritize tasks	68.8[a]	61.1**	54.6**	66.4
Gather information	62.6	60.1	52.5**	68.5**
Sort and categorize information	48.1	56.0[a]***	45.4	65.0**
Identify work-related problems	70.3[a]	58.3**	48.2**	67.1
Evaluation				
Identify potential solutions to problems	52.9	52.2	44.7	61.5**
Identify barriers to solutions	44.1	41.1	42.6	57.6**
Evaluate results	26.9	53.7[a]**	45.4**	62.6**
Leadership				
Problem-solve collaboratively or in teams	63.3	76.8[a]***	67.4	81.7**
Make decisions independently	35.2	75.3[a]***	66.7**	81.0**
Problem-solve in a leadership role	14.5	61.1[a]***	48.2**	68.6**
Implement solutions	31.7	57.3[a]***	52.5**	65.3**
Communication skill sets				
Customers				
Make and receive business phone calls	49.4	53.6	41.8	66.0**
Deal with customers	64.6[a]	55.4**	44.7**	64.8

Table 2.1 (continued)

New basic skills	Demand (% employers needing)	Supply (% employees who say they have) Low- and mid-skilled	Low-skilled	All
Customers				
Explain products and services	47.6	49.5	36.2**	59.6**
Handle complaints	47.4	45.7	34.0**	55.3**
Sell a product or service to a customer	28.4	42.1[a]**	36.9	49.5**
Coworkers				
Choose words and manner of expression appropriate at work	85.3[a]	50.3**	41.1**	61.5**
Be perceptive of verbal and nonverbal cues from others	81.5[a]	52.8**	46.1**	63.6**
Interact with coworkers to accomplish a task	90.8[a]	60.5**	45.4**	71.5**
Computer software skill sets				
Productivity enhancers				
Use word processing programs	27.4	26.0	22.7	39.4**
Use spreadsheet programs	20.4	18.3	14.9	28.4**
Use database software	17.2	15.0	11.3	23.5**
Use e-mail	23.2	36.1[a]**	27.0	51.9**
Use Internet browsers	16.0	34.9[a]**	26.2**	47.6**
Multimedia				
Use Web page/authoring software	1.7	9.4[a]**	7.1**	12.2**
Use multimedia authoring/editing software	1.0	7.1[a]**	5.0**	9.1**
Use graphics software	2.5	8.1[a]**	5.0**	12.6**
Use desktop publishing programs	1.5	10.4[a]**	6.4**	14.6**

Financial				
Use financial inventory software	3.0	6.9**	4.3	11.6**
Job equipment skill sets				
Office				
Use telephone systems (multiple lines)	63.6[a]	51.1**	41.8**	57.9
Use answering machines	37.9	63.9[a]**	53.2**	71.3**
Use copiers	44.9	62.1[a]**	46.1	70.7**
Use fax machines	42.1	44.5	29.1**	57.4**
Use Windows or DOS-based computers	34.2	28.8	20.6**	42.4**
Production				
Use production machinery	15.2	24.2[a]**	17.0	27.4**
Use heavy equipment	12.0	22.4[a]**	13.5	22.3**
N	402	393	141	672

NOTE: Data are from the BALS Employer (demand) and Household (supply) Surveys. "Low-skilled" is defined as having no more than a high school education *and* no more than one year of work experience. "Mid-skilled" is defined as having no more than a high school education *or* no more than one year of work experience. Numbers in the first column represent the percentage of employers stating that the skill is needed in the low-skilled job. Numbers in the remaining columns represent the percentage of individuals saying that they can execute the skill very well. ** indicates a statistically significant difference ($p \leq 0.05$) between supply and demand.

[a] In cases where that significant difference exists between the percentages in the first two columns, the placement of a superscript [a] in the first or second column indicates whether the demand for or the supply of entry- and mid-level workers is greater, as determined by a *t*-test.

SOURCE: Bay Area Longitudinal Surveys (HIRE 2006).

Prioritization skill set), only 48.2 percent of low-skilled workers said that they had that ability.

We constructed supply-side measures of an individual's skill set by mapping the skill questions in the Employer Survey to those in the Household Survey (Table A.1), a relatively straightforward process since the skill questions for employers mapped one-to-one to those for households, except in the area of English. Once skill measures for firms and individuals were mapped for consistency, we linked the measure of each skill in the Household Survey to the comparable skill in each skill set. Our supply-side measure of an individual's ability skill set was created by summing the number of skills that an individual held within a given skill set.[22]

Demand and Supply of Skills in the BALS Labor Market

The BALS data provide a unique opportunity to compare specific skills required in low-skilled positions in a local labor market against the supply of the same skills in the same local labor market. Such a comparison allows one to measure whether or not a particular skill (or set of skills) is difficult for firms to attract. Although we would like to measure the level of excess demand in the local labor market for each skill used in low-skilled positions, BALS does not have firm-level job vacancy and applicant flow information for this type of analysis. However, BALS does contain information about the skills required of workers in low-skilled jobs, allowing for a crude measure of demand. And it contains information about individuals' ability to execute similarly defined skills-based tasks, allowing for a crude measure of supply.

Comparing the parallel constructs for the skills employers need in low-skilled jobs and those possessed by workers affords us the opportunity of approximating the relative demand for each skill set. Specifically, we compare the percentage of low-skilled jobs (j) that use a specific skill with the percentage of individuals (i) with only a high school education or short-term work experience stating that they possess the skill, to approximate the level of relative demand for each skill (sk).[23] We use t-tests to compare the percentage of jobs requiring a particular skill (d_j^{sk}) to the percentage of the low and medium-skilled individuals in the BALS sample holding the same skill (s_i^{sk}).

Statistically significant differences ($p \leq 0.05$) between d_j^{sk} and s_i^{sk} suggest that a high relative demand ($d_j^{sk} > s_i^{sk}$ or $hd^{sk} = 1$, and 0 otherwise) or low relative demand ($d_j^{sk} < s_i^{sk}$ or $ld^{sk} = 1$, and 0 otherwise) exists for a particular skill. Skills with no significant difference in the proportions may be close to being in balance in the local labor market ($d_j^{sk} = s_i^{sk}$ or $e^{sk} = 1$, and 0 otherwise).

Clearly, few individuals enter the market with only one skill, and few jobs require only one skill. Instead, jobs require a set of skills, and individuals bring an array of skills to the labor market. A particular set of skills may contain some skills with a high relative demand and some with a low relative demand. We determine the relative demand for each skill set and classify each in mutually exclusive categories—high (relative) demand, low (relative) demand, and mixed demand—based on the dominance of skills of a given level of demand:

(2.1)   High D = 1 if $\dfrac{\sum\limits_{1}^{n} hd^{sk}}{\sum\limits_{1}^{n} ld^{sk} + \sum\limits_{1}^{n} e^{sk}} \geq 1$,

= 0 if otherwise;

(2.2)   Low D = 1 if $\dfrac{\sum\limits_{1}^{n} ld^{sk}}{\sum\limits_{1}^{n} hd^{sk} + \sum\limits_{1}^{n} e^{sk}} \geq 1$,

= 0 if otherwise;

(2.3)   Mixed D = 1 if High D = 0 and Low D = 0,

= 0 if otherwise;

where n is the number of individual skills in a particular skill set.

The plethora of skills held by low- and medium-skilled individuals produces a low relative demand for most skills required in entry-level, low-skilled jobs in the BALS local labor market (Table 2.1), including complex English, algebra, applied math, measurement, leadership, production equipment, multimedia, and financial software. The customer service, evaluation, productivity enhancement, and office equipment skill sets have some skills with high relative demand, some with low relative demand, and others with relatively equal proportions. Simple English, the ability to interact with coworkers, and prioritization have a high relative demand, suggesting that jobs using these skills will have higher wages if firms want to attract workers with needed skills (i.e., if our conventional model is incorrect).

Skills in the National Labor Market

We augment and support the analysis of skills in the BALS data with national data on skills in the Occupational Information Network (O*NET). O*NET 5.1 provides information on 974 occupations in the United States, 135 of which correspond to our definition of low-skilled jobs. O*NET draws information from job incumbent ratings of occupational tasks, skills, generalized work activities, knowledge, education and training, work styles, and the work setting. These are combined with analyst ratings of the abilities needed in each job.[24] Full-scale data collection efforts began in June 2001, and additional data has been gathered yearly on approximately 200 occupations in order to replenish the database every five years.[25] Information is collected using a two-stage design that identifies a statistically random sample of businesses expected to employ workers in the targeted occupations. Within those businesses, O*NET selects a random sample of workers in targeted occupations.

The 135 Job Zone 1 jobs in O*NET 5.1 are considered low-skilled jobs. Job Zone 1 jobs "may require a high school diploma or GED certificate," require "no previous work-related skill, knowledge, or experience," and provide "anywhere from a few days to a few months of training" (NCSC 2006). O*NET data allow us to provide a sweeping portrait of the general patterns of skills needed in low-skilled jobs. Such a picture enables us to compare broadly defined skill requirements in jobs requiring little formal education and work experience to those required in other types of jobs.[26]

The two databases permit verification of results using different levels of geography and different conceptual and empirical definitions of skills. This in turn makes possible a sensitivity analysis to establish how skills are used in low-skilled jobs. BALS affords us the opportunity to examine skills in low-skilled jobs within a local labor market, while O*NET allows us to look at skills in low-skilled jobs for the nation as a whole. By comparing the two levels of geography, we confirm the typicality of the BALS labor market with respect to skill usage in low-skilled jobs.

The definitions of skills in the two databases differ in two subtle but important ways. First, O*NET captures the intensity of using a skill in a job by measuring usage on a scale from 1 (lowest) to 7 (highest), while BALS measures skill use as a binary measure of whether or not the skill is used on the job. Second, because the BALS sample contains only jobs requiring no more than a high school education and one year of work experience, its skill measures are a relatively fine gradation of skills that might be used in low-skilled jobs. In contrast, the O*NET sample of jobs reflects jobs throughout the economy, and its skill measures are less targeted and less specified to low-skilled jobs than are the BALS skill measures (e.g., O*NET measures reading comprehension; BALS measures the reading of written instructions, memos, etc.). Comparing the results of analysis using the two definitions of skills allows us to verify results with differing constructs used to capture skills.

SUMMARY

Our conventional description of the labor market for workers in low-skilled jobs is driven by the supposition that the lack of skills needed by workers in such jobs makes workers a homogeneous commodity in the eyes of the employer and produces a competitive labor market for their services. With a seemingly inexhaustible supply of workers for low-skilled jobs, market forces will set wages and employment, and incumbent workers will have little job security and little chance to move beyond the entry-level, low-skilled job. This conventional description of the labor market for workers in low-skilled jobs stands in contrast to the labor market that develops for workers in jobs needing skills. Within such a market, workers become differentiated by their level of skills, and a market for skills develops. Individuals with skills in relatively short supply will earn increased wages, and firms will develop strategies for retaining workers with needed skills, including paying above-market wages and affording individuals an opportunity for career progression.

We use data from a local labor market in northern California, augmented by a national database on skills, to describe the market for workers in low-skilled positions and to compare its operation to that of our conventional description. Because California often serves as a bellwether for the nation in its ability to foreshadow political, economic, and demographic trends, the BALS local labor data are taken from a near-ideal venue for describing the operation of a local labor market for workers in low-skilled positions.

BALS contains extensive information on the skills that employers require in low-skilled positions, in addition to information on firms' recruiting and screening practices, compensation, and internal labor market structure. This information allows researchers to link skills, behavior, and employment outcomes for firms with available low-skilled positions. BALS also contains information about the skill levels of individuals residing in a low-income community in the BALS local labor market, allowing for a comparison of the relative demand for and supply of skills and a determination of whether skills with a high relative demand (i.e., skills in short supply) cause firms to behave in a manner that supports our conventional description of the labor market for workers in low-skilled positions.

Notes

1. We focus on dual labor market theory and not on dual economy theory because of the former's emphasis on jobs and occupations, which are the focus of our study.
2. Studies have shown that higher-educated workers increasingly have taken positions previously held by lesser-educated workers (Hecker 1992, 1995; Teulings and Koopmanschap 1989). During economic downturns, lower-educated workers are more likely to leave firms but are not necessarily replaced with higher-educated workers (Gautier et al. 2002; van Ours and Ridder 1995).
3. BALS results can be found at www.hire.csueastbay.edu/Hire/bals.htm (HIRE 2006).
4. Statistics in this section are drawn from the American Community Survey Profile (U.S. Census Bureau 2003b).
5. National homeowner vacancy rates stood at 1.7 percent, rental vacancy rates at 7.1 percent, and homeownership rates at 66.4 percent in 2002. Comparable rates in California were 1.2, 3.9, and 57.0 percent.
6. A copy of each of the BALS surveys can be found at http://www.hire.csueastbay.edu/Hire/bals.htm (HIRE 2006).

7. A more detailed description of the three-county area can be found at http://www .hire.csueastbay.edu/hire/discpap/abstracts/D04-06-04.pdf (Maxwell 2004a).

8. Eighty-one percent of the BALS questionnaires were completed in 2001–2002. Surveys to employers had a 75.2 percent screener response rate and a 21.4 percent response rate for firms eligible to participate. A description of the methods, including a comparison of BALS firms with those in the three-county area, is available at www.hire.csueastbay.edu/hire/discpap/abstracts/D04-06-04.pdf (Maxwell 2004a). This report shows that BALS jobs represent a smaller proportion of construction jobs than those available in the three-county area, as is consistent with the BALS requirement that jobs be available through an open application process.

9. Because BALS was designed to obtain information about currently available low-skilled job opportunities, the Employer Survey was administered to a firm only if that firm had job openings in low-skilled positions.

10. In all but 7 percent of the cases, one individual was able to answer both sets of questions.

11. BALS initially set a goal of completing the Employer Survey for 25 firms of each size (large, medium, and small) in each county; however, funding in Alameda County allowed for an oversampling of firms in this county.

12. We defined a firm as an entity that established criteria for hiring, compensation, and workplace rules. Thus a McDonald's (for example) run by corporate headquarters was classified as a large firm, whereas a McDonald's franchise, owned and run separately, was classified as a small firm. The critical distinction is that in the case of the first McDonald's a large corporation sets the compensation and terms of employment, and in the case of the second McDonald's a single proprietor (the franchisee) sets them.

13. In 1998, BALS targeted surveys at San Francisco County firms in growth sectors of the economy—business services, finance, health and social services, public utilities, and government. Thirty-five firms participated in the Phone Survey and 15 participated in the Employer Survey. This target was dropped in 1999, allowing for surveying in all sectors.

14. Unemployment hovered around 8 percent in San Joaquin County during Wave I surveying, a relatively tight labor market for that county.

15. The initial 327 firms were surveyed from October 2002 through March 2003; the additional 78 Alameda County firms, as well as firms not contacted during the earlier period, were surveyed from October through December 2003.

16. Only partial overlap exists in the way the Employer Survey and Household Survey were conducted. Some 19.3 percent of the Employer Survey forms were distributed at the same time as the Household Survey, 66.2 percent were distributed a year before the Household Survey, and 14.6 percent were distributed about three-and-a-half years before the Household Survey.

17. The Household Survey was administered in the 94544 zip code of Hayward, California, and had a 37.3 percent response rate. For a fuller description of the community see www.hire.csueastbay.edu/hire/discpap/abstracts/F04-01-01.pdf (Maxwell 2004b) or www.hire.csueastbay.edu/hire/discpap/abstracts/F03-11-08

.pdf (Maxwell 2004b). A description of the methods used for the Household Survey is available at www.hire.csueastbay.edu/hire/discpap/abstracts/D04-06-04.pdf (Maxwell 2004a). Included in this report is a sociodemographic comparison of BALS survey respondents to the population living in the area as identified in the 2000 census. This analysis illustrates the similarity in respondents' demographics and characteristics (e.g., renters, level of education) between the BALS Household Survey data and that of the census.

18. Numbers are the author's computations from the U.S. Census 2000 Public Use Microdata Sample (PUMS), the 0.05 sample (U.S. Census Bureau 2003c).

19. Although BALS contains 76 measures of skills, we used only 53 in this study. Specific skills were removed from analysis for three reasons. First, skills that were asked in only two of the three Bay Area counties were not used, to maximize sample size and provide geographic spread. Second, because our analysis required a one-to-one matching of skills demanded by employers with those supplied by individuals, we consolidated skills that were unique from the employer's view but similar from the individual's view (e.g., employers saw reading safety warnings, instructions, product labels, and invoices as different skills, whereas individuals saw them as the same reading skill). Third, we removed seven skills from analysis that were not discriminating measures in our factor analysis.

20. We used the criterion of 0.5 as a significant loading to identify skills in each set. Although a typical rule of thumb for identifying patterns in the factors is a loading greater than 0.3, we chose the more stringent criterion so as to bundle only the most closely related skills. A description of the methods used to build the 15 skill sets is available at www.hire.csueastbay.edu/hire/discpap/abstracts/D04-06-07 .pdf (Maxwell 2004c). The factor analysis used to construct the skill sets shows that each of the constructs explains between 61.3 (communication) and 70.3 percent (equipment) of the variation in the skill requirements.

21. A factor analysis produces an n by m matrix of correlations between the original variables and their factors, where n is the number of variables and m is the number of retained factors. The interpretation of the (rotated) factors is inferred from the size of the variable's loading (akin to the size of a simple correlation coefficient). Because we had no *a priori* expectation of the number of patterns in any of the original skill groups, we allowed the factor analysis to determine the number of factors that accounted for the observed covariation within each. We specified an oblique factor solution, which produces correlated extracted factors, since it seemed reasonable to assume correlation between the skills in each grouping. We identify only factors with eigenvalues exceeding one.

22. If individuals stated that they could execute a task using the skill very well, they were said to possess the skill. The number of skills possessed in each skill set was summed to measure the respondent's skill set. For example, the measurement skill set (math) contains two skills: performing simple measurements and using measurement instruments. If a respondent said he performed both skills very well, he had a 2 on the skill set. If he could only perform one of the skills very well, he received a 1. If he could do neither very well, he received a 0.

23. Because, as Chapter 5 will show, individuals with more than low-skilled creden-

tials hold low-skilled jobs, we draw supply-side information from individuals with either a high school education or one year or less of work experience in making this comparison.

24. O*NET data are based on several hundred rating scales in questionnaires completed by sampled workers. Questions were organized into four different questionnaires, each containing a different set of questions, with sampled job incumbents randomly assigned to complete one of the four questionnaires. All respondents completed a task questionnaire and provided some general demographic information. A fifth questionnaire, focusing on abilities, was completed by occupational analysts using updated information from incumbent workers.

25. Although BALS was begun before O*NET's initial distribution, both surveys were in the field in 2001–2002.

26. For a definition of individual measures in O*NET, see http://online.onetcenter .org/skills (O*NET 2006a) for skills and http://harvey.psyc.vt.edu/Documents/ ONETabilities.pdf (O*NET 2006b) for abilities.

3
How Skills Matter

If you have enough knowledge you can succeed; if you don't gain any knowledge you cannot. You need to research and find [out] more and more [and] move forward. Every day you have to learn more and more so you can get better and better so you can go ahead with others.
    —A low-wage worker's response when asked what it takes for people to make it on their own

Our conventional model suggests that skills do not matter in the market for workers in low-skilled jobs. Yet the data, case studies, and research in Chapter 1 suggest otherwise: they show the need for skills even in the lowest of the low-skilled jobs (Shipler 2004).

Casual observations merely confirm the data. Working on production lines can challenge mental and physical agility. Providing child care requires multitasking, patience, physical stamina, and knowledge of human development. Furthermore, the concept of skill requirements in relatively low-skilled positions resonates with our images of waitresses balancing trays of food and memorizing orders or of farm workers discerning between ripe and unripe grapes when harvesting. Reports of the skills needed in low-skilled jobs also resonate with customers who have at some time been irritated by misstocked store shelves, sloppily cleaned bathrooms, or security lapses that result in weapons making it on board airplanes. When we notice the talents of workers in low-skilled food service positions or acknowledge the security threats prevented by low-skilled security guards, we implicitly confirm the need for skills in low-skilled jobs.

Thus, a modest body of research and a large body of anecdotal evidence suggest that low-skilled jobs require skills—a seeming contradiction to the conventional model presented in Chapter 2. But if skills matter in low-skilled jobs, how is a firm's behavior affected? BALS employers suggest that the need for skills in low-skilled jobs may impinge on their ability to find qualified workers: 60 percent report difficulties in finding qualified applicants for low-skilled positions when

49

**Table 3.1 BALS Employers' Ability to Find Qualified Applicants
in Differing Labor Markets (% responding affirmatively)**

	Labor Market		
	Tight	Medium	Loose
Overabundance of workers	1.2	0.0	3.3
Not difficult to find workers	27.2	32.5	37.5**
Somewhat difficult to find workers	35.8	40.3	36.2
Very difficult to find workers	35.8	27.3	23.0
N	177	77	152

NOTE: A tight labor market is one with county-level unemployment rates between 2.2
and 4.2 percent. A medium labor market has unemployment rates between 4.7 and
5.9 percent, and a loose labor market has unemployment rates between 7.0 and 8.3
percent. ** indicates that statistical significance ($p \leq 0.05$) exists between tight and
other labor markets, as determined by a t-test.
SOURCE: BALS Employer Survey (HIRE 2006).

unemployment rates exceed 7.0 percent; of these, 36.2 percent say it
is somewhat difficult to find workers and 23 percent say it is very difficult to find qualified workers in such times. In other words, 6 in 10
employers face some degree of difficulty filling low-skilled positions
even in the slackest of markets (Table 3.1). One reason firms consistently face difficulties in finding qualified applicants is that they find it
difficult to locate individuals who possess the specific skills needed in
low-skilled jobs. If skills were irrelevant in low-skilled work, workers
would be homogeneous, and the ability to attract qualified applicants
for low-skilled positions would vary according to the number of available workers there were. Thus, skill shortages are one explanation for
why employers have such a hard time finding qualified applicants.

This chapter explores the possibility that skills are an integral part
of low-skilled work by examining firms' reported use of skills in such
work. It looks at the behavior of firms to determine whether the need for
skills moves the labor market for workers in low-skilled jobs away from
the conventional description and toward a market-for-skills model. If
the labor market for workers in low-skilled jobs is one of skills, we
might expect to see three things:

  1)   differences in skill usage in low-skilled jobs that vary system-
       atically across occupations and industries,

2) wages and training in low-skilled jobs that change with labor supply, and

3) increased wages in low-skilled jobs using skills that are in short supply in the labor market.

Skill differentiation in low-skilled jobs suggests that job duties and skill-set use will vary across occupations. Administration and office-support occupations may, for example, require workers to possess a relatively large number of reading, writing, and computer skills but not to possess math skills. In contrast, retail sales positions may require individuals to compute discounts but not require them to write or use a computer. We would also expect the demand for and use of skills to vary across industries, since skills are an input to a firm's production. For example, farming and mining jobs might use physical abilities but not English communication and math, while service-sector jobs might require workers to have communication skills to interact with customers, reading and writing skills to complete forms and invoices, and math skills to compute discounts.

Furthermore, if skills matter in low-skilled jobs, firms will vary wages and training according to the supply of available labor as they attempt to find needed skills. In tight labor markets, firms will increase wages as they bid up the price of skills and provide training to workers in low-skilled positions. Conversely, in loose labor markets, wages and training will decrease as firms' ability to attract skills increases.

Finally, if skills matter in low-skilled jobs, employers will increase wages in jobs using skills with a high relative demand (irrespective of the tightness of the labor market). That is, if firms cannot attract a sufficient number of workers who have a needed skill, wages in jobs using the skill will increase as firms compete for the relatively few workers with such skills by bidding up wages.

SKILL PATTERNS EXIST ACROSS OCCUPATIONS AND INDUSTRIES

Even a cursory view of the job duties entailed in BALS jobs (Table A.2) suggests that the types of skills needed vary by occupation. Workers use very different skills in creating artwork (e.g., multimedia artist and animator jobs), interviewing clients (medical and public-health social worker jobs), making pizza (cook and fast-food worker jobs), answering phones (host and hostess jobs), polishing metalwork (janitor and cleaner jobs), repairing termite damage (pest control jobs), supervising children's groups (child-care worker jobs), making change (counter and rental clerk jobs), handling complaints (retail sales jobs), setting up accounts (bookkeeping jobs), filing (receptionist jobs), loading and stocking merchandise (stock clerk jobs), preparing charts (data entry jobs), lifting (mail clerk and communication-equipment mechanic jobs), making house repairs (maintenance and repair jobs), assembling (production and assembly jobs), driving trucks (freight hauler jobs), and standing in a production line (hand packer and packaging jobs).

The perusal of job duties in low-skilled BALS jobs also suggests that skills are not used in isolation but are required in combinations that vary across occupations and industries, a proposition that we test using both O*NET and BALS data. The factor analysis of BALS data presented in Chapter 2 uncovered 15 skill sets used in low-skilled jobs. A factor analysis on skills in the O*NET database uncovered six distinct patterns of skill use (Table A.3), and these patterns generally confirmed the skill sets that had emerged from the BALS data. New basic skills emerged in three of the six factor loadings. We identify these new basic skills as the English communication, math, and problem-solving skill sets.

The most dominant factor, which accounted for 16.4 percent of the variation in skill requirements, contains English communication skills: reading comprehension, active listening, writing and speaking skills, and written and oral comprehension and expression abilities. Math skills are loaded on a separate factor, and math skills, number facility, and written expression all make up a math ability skill set. A problem-solving factor includes problem sensitivity, selective attention, time sharing, and reaction time abilities. Physical abilities separate into two identifiable factors, which we call large- and small-motor skill sets. The large-motor skills factor includes manual dexterity, extent of flexibility, static strength, multilimb coordination, trunk strength, speed of limb movement, and stamina abilities. The small-motor skills include near vision, information ordering, manual dexterity, wrist/finger speed, arm/hand scale, finger dexterity, visualization, and perceptual speed.

Another factor identifies mechanical skills, which include mechanical knowledge, operation and control, equipment selection, operation monitoring, quality control analysis, equipment maintenance, and control precision ability.

To ensure that the skill sets developed in each data set were not an artifact of that data set's sampling of jobs, we linked O*NET skill measures to BALS jobs through the SOC*ONET occupational code and applied a factor analysis to uncover skill patterns (Table A.4). The analysis confirms previous analysis. Math, large-motor, and small-motor skill sets are skill sets used in both O*NET and BALS low-skilled jobs. The BALS sample with O*NET skills analysis did produce two slight differences in the remaining two skill sets: first, the English, communication, and problem-solving skill sets combined to form a single set of skills in the BALS data; second, a set of "assembly" (as in working on an assembly line) skills emerged.

Evidence therefore is fairly strong that low-skilled jobs require basic (English, math, communication, and problem-solving) or job-specific (physical and mechanical ability) skill sets. It is less clear, however, that the computer skills identified by Murnane and Levy (1996) are an identifiable skill set widely used in low-skilled jobs, at least at the entry level.

The question is, "Do these skill sets vary systematically across occupations or industries?" If skill sets were used in about the same proportion in all low-skilled jobs, little correlation would exist between skills and occupational or industrial wages, as our conventional model posits, even if skills were related to productivity or job performance.

We use the average factor score for each skill set to approximate the level of skills required in it and then compare the factor score (i.e., the measure of the intensity of skill set usage) across occupations or industries. If no skill set differences exist across industries or occupations, all factor scores will be close to zero. If a factor score is positive and relatively high (as compared to the factor score in other occupations or industries), it indicates that the skill set is used extensively in the occupation or industry. If it is negative, it indicates that the skill set is not used in the occupation or industry.

To ensure consistency in our conclusions across different definitions of skills and databases, we analyze occupational differences using BALS data, O*NET data, and O*NET skills linked to BALS jobs, as we did in our analysis of skill patterns.[1] We focus on skill differences among the six occupations (food, building and grounds maintenance, office, production, sales, and transportation) and three industries (services, manufacturing, and retail trade) that have the most employment opportunities for workers in low-skilled jobs. The analysis shows that low-skilled occupations require different skill sets (Table 3.2), a result that is robust across databases (O*NET and BALS). Jobs in office work and administrative support require the highest level of skills, followed by jobs in sales. Administrative support jobs require relatively high levels of simple and complex English, applied math, algebra, prioritization and evaluation, leadership, communication with customers and coworkers, and office equipment skill sets (using the finer gradations of skill sets in the BALS data). Sales occupations require simple English, applied math, algebra, ability to evaluate, communication with customers, and office equipment skills.

Positions in production, maintenance, and transportation require fewer skills than administrative support or sales positions, but they do require physical and mechanical skills and abilities (Table 3.2). Production jobs require mechanical skills, small motor abilities, and math and problem-solving abilities, while maintenance and transportation positions require measurement skills and large motor abilities. Jobs in production, maintenance, and transportation all use production equipment skills. Food service positions require the fewest skills of all occupations with low-skilled positions, although they do require large motor coordination skills.

Industrial differences also emerge (Table 3.3). The service sector houses jobs requiring the highest level of skills: medical and education establishments have positive and relatively high factor scores in 11 of the 15 skill sets, indicating that jobs in this sector use simple and complex English, algebra and measurement, communication with customers and coworkers, prioritizing and leadership, productivity-enhancing and multimedia software, and office equipment skills. Jobs in services other than business, medical, and education require 10 of the 15 skill sets: simple and complex English; applied math and measurement; communication with customers and coworkers; prioritizing, evaluating, and leadership; and office equipment usage. The only skills not used in this sector are computer software skills, algebra, and production equipment usage. Jobs in the business service sector use 10 of the 15 skill sets: simple and complex English, communication with customers and coworkers, evaluation and prioritizing of problem-solving, productivity enhancers, multimedia and financial software, and office equipment usage. Of note, entry-level, low-skilled jobs in the business service sector do not require math or leadership skills, perhaps owing to their entry-level nature. Positions above entry level may well require their use, a proposition examined in Chapter 5. Jobs in retail trade require relatively low levels of skills but do require communication with customers and coworkers and applied math skills. Jobs in manufacturing use production equipment and math skills.[2]

WAGES AND TRAINING DO NOT CHANGE WITH LABOR MARKET CHANGES

The variety of skills used in low-skilled jobs, the frequency with which skills are required, and the systematic use of different skills across occupations and industries all suggest that skills are an important element of low-skilled jobs. But are they important enough to alter a firm's behavior such that wages or training increase during labor shortages (i.e., when unemployment levels are low)? Because the BALS data was initiated during tight labor markets, when county unemployment rates were between 2.2 and 4.2 percent, and continued through loose labor markets, when county unemployment rates were 7.0 percent and above, we can determine whether firms vary compensation and training with fluctuations in labor supply.

Our analysis suggests that firms' compensation and training levels vary little with changes in labor supply (Table 3.4). Wages, the offer of fringe benefits, and the offer of medical benefits do not vary significantly between tight and loose labor markets. Neither does the provision of training. In fact, the only compensation or training component that varies with labor supply is overtime pay: firms are more likely to pay overtime in a loose labor market, perhaps in lieu of hiring permanent workers (McMenamin, Krantz, and Krolik 2003).

Table 3.2 Occupational Differences in Skill Use in Low-Skilled Jobs

	Food	Building/ grounds maintenance	Office	Production	Sales	Transport.	Other occupation
O*NET data and skills							
New basics							
English communication	−0.120	−0.830	0.908[a]	−0.546	1.251[a]	0.057	0.060
Math	−0.397	−0.753	0.478[a]	0.359[a]	0.528[a]	−0.441	−0.469
Problem-solving	−0.825	−0.625	−0.388	0.211[a]	0.313[a]	0.032	0.149[a]
Mechanical and physical							
Mechanical	−1.144	−0.219	−0.737	0.792[a]	−1.265	0.283[a]	−0.250
Large motor	0.221[a]	1.314[a]	−1.021	−0.043	−0.728	0.500[a]	0.359[a]
Small motor	−0.245	−0.348	−0.267	0.637[a]	−0.614	−0.352	−0.324
% occupational distribution in O*NET	6.7	2.2	14.8	34.1	4.4	13.3	24.5
N	9	3	20	46	6	18	33
BALS data and skills							
English							
Simple English	−0.618	−0.793	0.426[a]	−0.471	0.163[a]	−0.120	0.089
Complex English	−0.598	−0.545	0.571[a]	−0.522	0.052	−0.545	0.062
Math							
Applied math	0.050	−0.786	0.231[a]	−0.536	1.114[a]	−0.378	−0.326
Algebra	−0.448	−0.505	0.255[a]	−0.018	0.290[a]	−0.289	−0.058
Measurement	−0.106	0.092[a]	−0.170	0.210	0.044[a]	−0.245	0.298[a]

57

Problem-solving							
Prioritization	-0.377	-0.353	0.359[a]	-0.460	0.032	-0.158	0.015
Evaluation	-0.408	-0.374	0.107[a]	-0.168	0.202[a]	-0.188	0.220[a]
Leadership	-0.144	-0.279	0.122[a]	-0.149	0.026	-0.002	0.037
Communication							
Customers	0.026	-0.678	0.367[a]	-1.042	0.921[a]	-0.453	-0.138
Coworkers	-0.313	-0.206	0.242[a]	-0.374	0.009	-0.028	-0.011
Computer							
Productivity enhancers	-0.591	-0.630	0.787[a]	-0.457	-0.126	-0.498	-0.231
Multimedia	-0.088	-0.164	0.076	-0.078	-0.029	-0.162	0.133[a]
Financial	-0.189	-0.196	0.203[a]	-0.229	0.037	-0.198	0.027
Job equipment							
Office	-0.632	-0.807	0.872[a]	-0.774	0.080[a]	-0.681	-0.139
Production	-0.270	0.248[a]	-0.313	1.082[a]	-0.389	0.559[a]	-0.104
% occupational distribution in BALS	8.0	8.0	32.4	10.5	12.5	10.5	18.2
N	32	32	130	42	50	42	73
BALS data and O*NET skills							
New basics							
Communication and problem-solving	-0.897	-1.171	0.553[a]	-0.578	0.360[a]	-0.963	0.570[a]
Math	-0.730	-1.106	0.514[a]	-0.365	0.988[a]	0.501[a]	-0.345
Mechanical and physical							
Mechanical	-0.880	0.342[a]	-0.277	1.308[a]	-1.008	0.423[a]	0.453[a]
Large motor	0.319[a]	1.086[a]	-0.921	0.710[a]	0.062	0.627[a]	0.275[a]

(continued)

Table 3.2 (continued)

	Food	Building/ grounds maintenance	Office	Production	Sales	Transport.	Other occupation
Small motor	-0.200	0.098	-0.033	0.921[a]	-0.058	-0.383	-0.188
Assembly	0.308[a]	-0.323	0.081	0.576[a]	-0.788	0.041	0.034
% occupational distribution in BALS	8.0	7.8	33.3	10.8	12.5	10.5	17.0
N	32	31	133	43	50	42	68

NOTE: Numbers represent the average factor score in each occupation.
[a] Indicates relatively large, positive factor scores across occupations. BALS did not contain skill information for three occupations. O*NET did not contain skill information for six occupations in the BALS data set.
SOURCE: O*NET (NCSC 2006); BALS Employer Survey (HIRE 2006).

SKILLS WITH HIGH RELATIVE DEMAND
INCREASE WAGES

At least two explanations exist for compensation and training remaining constant in the face of changes in labor supply. First, firms might target their efforts at attracting specific skills that they have difficulty obtaining. In this type of case, wages may not fluctuate with changes in labor supply as much as they change with relative demand for specific skills. Second, firms might use skill requirements as screens for employment. In this type of case, skills may not actually be required for task performance and are, instead, used to establish minimal standards in hiring. These explanations are not mutually exclusive. We examine the first explanation in the remaining portion of this chapter and the second in the next chapter.

Let's suppose that firms do not value all skills equally—a supposition that an aggregate analysis of labor supply ignores. Our analysis thus far supports such a supposition by showing a wide variety in the skills required for low-skilled jobs and in skill differences among occupations and industries. The heterogeneity in skills makes the demand for skills multidimensional and raises the possibility that skill bottlenecks can exist in low-skilled jobs even in the face of labor surpluses. In such cases, wages would increase in jobs requiring skills for which an excess demand exists, even if the unemployment rate suggests that there are labor surpluses. It is not difficult to imagine a scenario in which a bottleneck exists for a particular skill required in a relatively large number of low-skilled jobs, say, English communication or applied math. In such an instance, aggregate levels of wages and of training for workers in low-skilled positions would be impervious to fluctuations in the labor supply because increased wages and training are a constant in jobs using English or math.

A cursory examination of the wages paid in different occupations suggests that the skill differences across occupations translate into wage differences, with jobs in the occupations that require the highest level of skills generally paying the highest wages (Table 3.5). Thus, office positions, which require the highest level of skills, average $10.21 an hour, about three dollars an hour more than the $7.34 paid in food service jobs, which require the lowest level of skills. Wage dispersion exists

Table 3.3 Differences in Skill Requirements by Industry Sector (%)

	Services			Manufacturing	Retail trade	Other industries
	Business	Education & medical	Other			
New basic skill sets						
English reading and writing						
Simple English	0.121[a]	0.286[a]	0.025[a]	−0.400	−0.138	0.118[a]
Complex English	0.249[a]	0.137[a]	0.117[a]	−0.408	−0.236	0.160[a]
Math						
Algebra	−0.062	0.066[a]	−0.113	−0.118	−0.081	0.216[a]
Applied math	−0.182	−0.094	0.114[a]	−0.440	0.421[a]	−0.097
Measurement	−0.244	0.267[a]	0.107[a]	0.018[a]	−0.179	0.077[a]
Problem-solving						
Prioritization	0.224[a]	0.276[a]	0.096[a]	−0.350	−0.140	−0.003
Evaluation	0.167[a]	−0.031	0.201[a]	−0.077	−0.210	0.028
Leadership	−0.288	0.066[a]	0.225[a]	−0.246	−0.015	0.107[a]
Communication						
Customers	0.135[a]	0.058[a]	0.141[a]	−0.867	0.402[a]	−0.112
Coworkers	0.134[a]	0.158[a]	0.176[a]	−0.201	0.038[a]	−0.199
Computer software						
Productivity enhancers	0.220[a]	0.369[a]	−0.163	−0.337	−0.276	0.251[a]
Multimedia	0.458[a]	0.138[a]	−0.149	−0.136	−0.086	−0.052
Financial	0.063[a]	−0.083	−0.003	0.007	−0.021	0.026[a]

Job equipment skill sets						
Office equipment	0.286[a]	0.382[a]	0.073[a]	−0.608	−0.281	0.197[a]
Production equipment	−0.057	−0.281	−0.203	0.768[a]	−0.311	0.194[a]
% employment	12.5	12.0	16.5	12.7	22.4	23.9
N	50	48	66	51	90	96

NOTE: Industrial information is not available in O*NET. Numbers represent the average factor score in each industry.
[a] Indicates relatively large, positive factor scores across industries.
SOURCE: BALS Employer Survey (HIRE 2006).

Table 3.4 Compensation and Training Offered by Firms in Different Labor Markets (% employers responding affirmatively)

	Labor Market		
	Tight	Medium	Loose
Compensation			
Hourly rate of pay ($)	9.43	9.27	9.54
Do not offer benefits	14.8	11.7	13.8
Offer medical benefits	80.7	81.8	77.6
Offer overtime	35.2	80.5**	78.3**
Do not provide training	62.8	55.8	64.9
N	176	77	152

NOTE: A tight labor market is one with a county-level unemployment rate between 2.2 and 4.2 percent. A medium labor market has an unemployment rate between 4.7 and 5.9 percent, and a loose labor market has an unemployment rate between 7.0 and 8.3 percent. ** indicates statistical significance ($p \leq 0.05$) exists between tight and other labor markets, as determined by t-tests. N varies slightly with item-specific nonresponse.
SOURCE: BALS Employer Survey (HIRE 2006).

within occupations, however. Over 20 percent of the jobs in administrative support pay less than $7.87 an hour, whereas 54.9 percent pay $10 or more an hour. In contrast, over 75 percent of food service jobs pay less than $7.87 an hour, and only about 6 percent pay $10 or more an hour.

The general relationship between pay and skill level in jobs is broken for jobs in sales. Despite having skill requirements similar to those in administrative support jobs, sales jobs pay wages significantly lower on average ($8.66 an hour compared to $9.44). More than half of all sales jobs pay less than $7.87 an hour.

A disconnect also exists in the skills-wage relationship because the ability of wages to reach $15 an hour does not correlate with occupations' skill levels (Table 3.5). In fact, if a job has above-average starting wages (e.g., an office job), it has an above-average probability of having wages reach $15 an hour. The converse is also true. Both the inconsistency between wages and skill requirements in sales jobs and the seeming correlation between starting wages and wage mobility in all low-skilled jobs suggest that forces other than skills may determine wages in low-skilled positions, a proposition that we will subsequently take up.

Table 3.5 Wage Differential by Type of Skill, Occupation

	Total	New basic skills		Physical and mechanical skills			Few skills	
		Office	Sales	Production	Transportation	Bldg./grds. maintenance	Food	Other occupation
Wages								
% low wages ($5.15–$7.87)	33.0	21.1**	56.3**	29.2	20.9*	29.4	75.8**	31.2
% medium wages ($8.00–$9.97)	30.3	24.1	22.9	43.8	44.2	32.4	18.2*	34.4
% high wages ($10.00+)	36.8	54.9**	20.8**	27.1	34.9	38.2	6.1**	34.4
% in top 12% of wages ($13.00+)	12.0	14.3	2.1**	12.5	11.6	20.6	3.0**	14.8
% reach $15/hour	40.7	51.6**	36.4	43.8	46.5	41.2	3.1**	33.9
Mean wage ($)	9.44	10.21**	8.06**	9.10	9.70	9.88	7.34**	9.83
(Standard deviation)	(3.00)	(2.68)	(1.76)	(2.66)	(3.45)	(3.24)	(1.63)	(3.85)
N	405	134	49	49	43	34	33	63
% N of total	100	33.1	12.1	12.1	10.6	8.4	8.1	15.6

NOTE: N varies slightly within the cells with item-specific response. ** indicates significant ($p \leq 0.05$) differences exist between the total and the specific occupation, as determined by a t-test.

SOURCE: BALS Employer Survey (HIRE 2006).

For now, we will focus on the skills-wage relationship and argue that the ability of skills to increase wages depends on their relative scarcity in the labor market. On the one hand, if firms have little difficulty attracting workers who possess a needed skill, wages will remain at market levels for workers with that skill. On the other hand, if firms cannot attract sufficient workers who have a needed skill, wages in the jobs using that skill will increase as firms compete for the relatively few workers with that particular skill. As a result, a skill with a high relative demand in a labor market (conceptually, a skill for which demand exceeds supply) will increase wages in jobs using the skill ($\alpha > 0$ in Equation [3.1] below), an assertion we test by estimating the general form

(3.1) $W_j = \alpha_0 + Skills_j\alpha + Inst_j\beta + \gamma LM + \varepsilon$,

where

W = a measure of compensation in the low-skilled job (j);
$Skills$ = a vector of skill sets used in the low-skilled job;
$Inst$ = a vector of variables describing the firm, including size, industrial sector, and unionization in the low-skilled job;
LM = the county's unemployment rate during the month of surveying; and
ε = the error term.

(Table A.5 provides the empirical specification of all variables.)[3] In this analysis, the factor scores discussed in Chapter 2 are used as skill set measures (*Skills*) in low-skilled positions (j). We use skill set measures from both BALS and O*NET (in separate analyses), which allows for a sensitivity analysis of whether results change with different measures of skills.

Because wage increases could be manifested in either starting or future wages, we estimate Equation (3.1) with two measures of wages, expecting that demand pressures could be exerted in one of two ways. The first measure is the log of hourly rate of pay in the entry-level job (log$W$), which captures a point-in-time estimate of wages. Because log$W$ is a continuous measure, we use ordinary least squares in its estimation. The second measure, which is whether or not the wages in the initial position can ever reach $15 an hour in the job, is binary and captures the potential for wages to grow in the job. We use logit analysis for its estimation. Interpreting the coefficients on skill measures (α) allows us to assess the significance of the relationship between a particular skill and wages, but it does not allow us to assess whether skills or institutional factors (*Inst*) dominate in setting occupational wages in low-skilled jobs, a query raised by the descriptive analysis in Table 3.5. The relative strength of each individual influence (e.g., individual skill or whether or not the firm is large) is determined by comparing the absolute size of the standardized coefficients in OLS estimations of the log wages and the log odds in logit estimations of wage mobility. The relative strength of all skills (*Skills*) and all institutional influences (*Inst*) is determined by comparing the incremental R^2 value upon entrance of each set of variables.

The multivariate analysis suggests that skills with a high relative demand in the local labor market increase wages (Table 3.6). Simple English, productivity enhancers, and office equipment skill sets, all of which have at least some skills with a high relative demand, increase starting wages. As well, jobs using priority and productivity enhancer skill sets have a higher probability of wages reaching $15 an hour, presumably if the worker demonstrates skills on the job. Only two skill sets have a significant relationship with wages that is potentially inconsistent with the proposition that skills with a high relative demand increase wages: customer service and production equipment. One explanation for this inconsistency is a correlation between unmeasured factors, measured skills, and wages. We examine this possibility by comparing the characteristics of jobs that use high levels of each skill set, defined as factor scores greater than 1.0 (Table 3.7). Of primary interest in this analysis is determining whether jobs using customer service and production equipment skill sets have characteristics that might account for the inconsistent wage-skill relationship.

The results are very revealing. Jobs using high levels of customer service skills, which have a mixed demand for skills but a negative relationship with wages, have a significantly lower proportion of jobs covered by a union. In fact, only 0.1 percent of such jobs have union representation. In contrast, jobs requiring high levels of production equipment skills, which have a low relative demand but a positive relationship with wages, have a significantly higher proportion (40 percent) of jobs covered by a union. These results suggest that unobservable

66

Table 3.6 Occupational Wage Coefficients by Skills and Institutional Factors

	Level of demand	BALS skills		O*NET skills	
		Log wage	Reach $15/hr.	Log wage	Reach $15/hr.
New basic skill sets					
English					
Simple English	High D	0.146***	1.225	—	—
Complex English	Low D	0.071*	0.814	—	—
Math					
Applied math	Low D	−0.101	0.905	—	—
Algebra	Low D	0.022	0.957	—	—
Measurement	Low D	0.013	1.062	—	—
Problem-solving					
Prioritization	High D	0.056	1.422**	—	—
Evaluation	Mixed D	−0.003	1.189	—	—
Leadership	Low D	−0.016	0.800	—	—
Communication					
Customers	Mixed D	−0.147**	0.879	—	—
Coworkers	High D	0.054	1.129	—	—
Computer software					
Productivity enhancers	Mixed D	0.182***	1.501**	—	—
Multimedia software	Low D	0.011	1.102	—	—
Financial software	Low D	−0.014	0.960	—	—
Job equipment skill sets					
Office equipment	Mixed D	0.157**	1.333	—	—

	Low D				
Production equipment		0.101**	1.280*	—	—
O*NET skills					
Communication and problem-solving				0.120**	1.140
Math				0.076	1.372**
Mechanical				0.158***	1.393**
Large motor				−0.055	0.965
Small motor				−0.098*	1.145
Assembly				−0.049	0.868
Institutional					
Small firm	—	−0.008	1.449	−0.063	1.326
Large firm	—	0.066	2.453***	0.088*	2.870****
Service industry	—	−0.102**	0.426**	−0.136**	0.443**
Manufacturing industry	—	−0.122**	0.633	−0.149***	0.516*
Retail trade industry	—	−0.190****	0.754	−0.303****	0.583
Business service industry	—	−0.098**	0.733	−0.126**	0.788
Education and medical industries		−0.073	0.523	−0.071	0.736
Union		0.315****	1.645*	.337****	1.753**
Mean dependent variable		2.20	.407	2.20	.404
N		393	381	390	379

NOTE: Numbers represent the standardized coefficients from ordinary least squares (Log wage) or odds ratios (Reach $15/hr.) from logit estimations. VIF's never exceed 3.3. Table A.5 provides a definition of all variables. Full results are available from the author. **** $p \leq 0.001$; *** $p \leq 0.01$; ** $p \leq 0.05$; * $p \leq 0.10$. An em dash (—) = data not available. Blank = not applicable.
SOURCE: BALS Employer Survey (HIRE 2006).

Table 3.7 BALS Jobs That Use Each Skill Set, by Demographic (%)

	Union	Female	Black	Asian	Latino	N
All jobs	26.7	55.9	13.2	4.0	19.2	399
Jobs using the customer service skill set	0.1**	66.9	12.4	3.9	12.9	86
Jobs using the production equipment skill set	40.0**	28.4	13.2	4.1	24.2	85
Jobs using the simple English skill set	—	—	—	—	—	—
Jobs using the prioritization skill set	27.7	62.9	12.6	3.9	15.0	66
Jobs using the productivity enhancers skill set	24.4	76.9	12.6	3.9	13.7	80
Jobs using the office equipment skill set	27.8	79.0	12.6	4.0	13.6	99

NOTE: Numbers show, by demographic, the percentage of BALS jobs that use each skill set, defined as those having a factor score that is greater than one. For simplicity in presentation, results are presented only for skill sets that are significantly related to wages or mobility. Asterisks indicate a significant ($p \leq 0.05$) difference between all jobs and jobs using specific skills, as indicated by a t-test. Jobs using the simple English skill set show em dashes instead of numbers because there were no observations made in this skill set.

SOURCE: BALS Employer Survey (HIRE 2006).

characteristics of jobs requiring customer service and production equipment skills, which also are associated with unionization, may drive wage-setting in the jobs using customer communication and production equipment. For example, industries using production equipment have an increased risk of nonfatal injury (BLS 2005), which may be correlated with increased wages and the propensity of the job to have union representation. It might be that compensating differentials for increased risk, which is an unobserved characteristic of firms housing jobs that use production equipment skills, drives the positive correlation between production equipment skills and occupational wages.

Analysis presented thus far suggests that wages increase in jobs using skills with a high relative demand. It also suggests that institutional factors influence wages. When we compare standardized coefficients (Table 3.6), we see that the influence of unions on wages is more than one-and-a-half times as great as that of productivity enhancing, office equipment, simple English, or production equipment skills (0.315, compared to 0.182, 0.157, 0.146, and 0.101). The negative influence of employment in the retail, manufacturing, and service sectors is nearly as strong (−0.190, −0.122, −0.102) as the positive influence of those skills. While the influence of a particular institutional factor—like unionization—may be stronger than the influence of a particular skill set in setting wages, policies are often grounded in building either skills or institutions as a whole and are not necessarily focused on building a particular skill or institution. In this respect, it is important to know whether skill sets or institutions as a group have a stronger influence on wages, a query we answer using the incremental value R^2. When skill sets are entered as a single influence into log wage estimations containing institutional and labor market characteristics, the R^2 value increases by 0.160. When institutional characteristics are entered into an estimation containing skill sets and labor market characteristics, R^2 increases by 0.137. The influence of the variable *Union* alone raises the R^2 value by 0.075. All changes in R^2 are significant at $p \leq 0.001$. These results suggest that the influence of skills on occupational wages in low-skilled jobs is only slightly stronger than the influence of institutional factors, and that a union's influence accounts for about half of the institutional effect.

SUMMARY AND CONCLUSIONS

Arguably the most important inconsistency with our conventional model of homogeneous workers in low-skilled positions is the continued difficulty that firms face in locating qualified applicants for low-skilled positions. Even when area unemployment rates were above 7 percent, close to six in ten of BALS firms had difficulty—and one in four of them of them had extreme difficulty—finding qualified workers for low-skilled positions. Why would employers have difficulty recruiting qualified applicants in times of labor surpluses? Analysis presented in this chapter suggests that the answer is that skill bottlenecks exist in low-skilled jobs.

The analysis shows that a wide variety of skills and skill sets are required in low-skilled jobs, as even a casual perusal suggests. Mentally compare the jobs of multimedia artists, surveyors, fast-food cooks, receptionists, janitors, pest control workers, child care workers, retail sales clerks, stock clerks, equipment mechanics, maintenance and repair workers, production and assembly workers, truck drivers, and hand packers and packagers. Few of us would characterize these workers in low-skilled positions as having similar skills.

While the analysis supports the general statement that skills matter, the preponderance of evidence suggests that some skills matter more than others. At the most basic level, skills with a high relative demand in the labor market increase wages in low-skilled jobs. This finding suggests that workers in low-skilled jobs using skills in short supply will enjoy higher wages. It is not difficult to imagine a scenario in which a bottleneck exists for a particular skill. Because of the bottleneck, wages paid to workers with that skill would be impervious to fluctuations in the labor supply, since constant shortages exist for the skill.

The analysis also suggests that skill requirements differ tremendously along industrial and occupational lines, with jobs in the service sector requiring the highest level of skills. Specifically, low-skilled jobs in business, medical, and education firms require the most skills; these jobs call on workers to use English, math, communication, prioritizing and leadership, productivity enhancing software, and office equipment skills. Jobs in services other than business, medical, and education also require high levels of skills in English, applied math, communication, office equipment usage, prioritizing, evaluating, and leadership. Jobs in the business service sector use English, communication, evaluation and prioritizing, problem-solving, productivity enhancers and multimedia software, and office equipment skills. Jobs in retail trade require relatively low levels of skills but do require communication with customers and coworkers and applied math skills. Jobs in manufacturing use production equipment and math skills.

Skill differences also exist along occupational lines. Jobs in administrative support occupations require a relatively high level of new basic skills. Office administration jobs require relatively high levels of English, applied math, algebra, prioritizing, evaluation, leadership, communication, and office equipment skills (using the finer gradations of skill sets in the BALS data). Sales occupations require English, applied math, algebra, measurement, evaluation, communicating with customers, and office equipment skills. Positions in production, maintenance, and transportation require use of production equipment but relatively few of the new basic skills (English, math, problem-solving, communication, and computer software). Production jobs require mechanical and small-motor skills, math, and problem-solving abilities, while maintenance and transportation positions require measurement and large-motor skills. Food service jobs require large-motor skills.

Taken as a whole, our analysis suggests that the conventional description of a competitive labor market, in which firms compete for homogeneous workers, is not consistent with the actions of firms hiring workers in low-skilled jobs. Given the heterogeneity in skills required in low-skilled jobs, the demand for workers' skills becomes multidimensional and skill bottlenecks increase wages even in the face of labor surpluses.

The one anomaly in this scenario of skills and wages is the relatively strong influence on occupational wages of a union, a particular sector of employment, or a large firm. In fact, the overall effect of these institutional factors on wages is only slightly less than that of skills. Although the more highly skilled of the low-skilled workers are more likely to be placed in high-wage firms (Holzer, Lane, and Vilhuber 2004), the correlation is not perfect. Because institutional factors can increase wages, the luck of the draw in employment opportunities may come into play, and low-skilled workers could land in a firm in which the environment offsets their skills in determining their wages. This finding suggests that policies designed to increase the wages of low-skilled workers by skill-building may have their effects somewhat tempered by the placement of a worker's employment.

Notes

1. Industry codes are not available in O*NET; hence, we cannot use O*NET for this analysis.
2. Jobs outside the three industries hiring the majority of low-skilled, entry-level workers have positive and relatively high factor scores in five of the 15 skill sets: simple English, complex English, algebra, productivity-enhancing software, and office equipment.
3. Ideally, we would estimate a similar set of equations on the supply side with appropriate interactions between skills and occupations. Unfortunately, BALS contains too few respondents working in each occupational category for this analysis.

4

Recruiting and Screening Workers in Low-Skilled Positions

Working at a nonprofit I have gotten the chance to teach young people [about] resumes and job searches. I was amazed [at] how little they knew about presentations—meaning presenting themselves—on interview skills, and [on] how to use correct grammar.
    —A low-wage worker

Firms must attract applicants before they can hire for a low-skilled position, and analysis presented thus far suggests that firms will want to attract workers with appropriate skills. Attracting applicants with the skills needed for the job requires that firms design recruiting and screening methods to ferret out the appropriately skilled applicants. In an ideal world, firms could accurately assess each applicant's skills using readily available information. In the real world, recruiting, screening, and obtaining accessible information about the skills an applicant possesses are costly. Profit-maximizing firms must weigh these costs against the gains in productivity to be had from hiring an appropriately skilled worker. If individuals can quickly learn required skills, a profit-maximizing firm will use low-cost recruiting and screening tools, since the cost of developing needed skills is low. Alternatively, if skills form an integral part of the job and are not easily learned on the job, firms will use more sophisticated, and costly, recruiting and screening methods to identify applicants with needed skills.

One indication that firms use recruiting and screening tools to attract appropriately skilled workers is that they strive to obtain accurate information prior to hiring, even when the positions are low-skilled. In fact, assessing the quality of information received on applicants seems to be of paramount importance to employers of low-skilled workers: as they dig through such information, they view information from outside sources (e.g., schools or former employers) as suspect and rely on direct evidence collected from applicants, such as interviews and tests

(Rosenbaum 2001).[1] Firms consciously add richness to their pool of low-skilled workers (and save about one-third of their screening costs) by relying heavily on friends of employees when recruiting (Fernandez, Castilla, and Moore 2000). Both sets of behavior suggest that employers might be seeking direct evidence of specific skills needed on the job when they screen applicants for low-skilled jobs.

One possible way of screening applicants to get workers in the low-skilled job who possess the required skills is to use educational credentials or work experience, and then to develop targeted screening tools to find applicants with needed skills. In such cases, education may not be valued for the academic skills it imparts but for the signal it sends about an individual's ability to execute tasks needed in the job.[2] Under such conditions, employers' complaining about a lack of academic skills in workers without providing training for them or even looking at their high school transcripts may not be a mere excuse put forward by employers who do not really need skills but may instead be their attempt to verbalize that they find a lack of specific skills in their applicant pool (Boesel and Fredland 1999; Cappelli 1992; Holzer 1996; Zemsky 1994). That is, employers simply may use education as an initial screen in recruiting applicants and may be expressing discontent with the quality of academic skills of applicants in the pool because they cannot find individuals with the specific skills needed in the job (Maxfield 1988).[3]

Education may provide employers with a low-cost screen to weed out many individuals that cannot perform effectively; employers may then use more direct measurers of skills as a second-stage screen to find needed skills. If firms search for workers that have the skills needed in the low-skilled job, as opposed to using skills to screen applicants, recruiting and screening methods will be correlated with specific skills. If, however, firms simply want a filter for sifting through applicants, the recruiting methods and screens (e.g., education and work experience) will be loosely tied, at best, to the skills stated as needed in the job.

Skills required in the job are but one factor that might influence the recruiting and screening methods firms develop. Firm characteristics and scarcity of labor are others (Baron, Davis-Blake, and Bielby 1986). Large firms are more likely to engage in an extensive search for workers with needed skills; the scope of such a search generates a rich and large pool of applicants. Large firms benefit from attracting a rich applicant pool because they must have individuals whose work needs little monitoring, given the relative autonomy of workers in large organizations.[4] Economies of scale in production and recruiting may make it feasible for such firms to bear the expense of an extensive search.

Firms will also adapt recruiting and screening methods to changes in the supply of labor. Firms searching for workers in loose labor markets will receive a relatively large number of applications, even if they do not use extensive recruiting methods, simply because a relatively large number of individuals are looking for work. Firms therefore will be able to use less extensive (or fewer) recruiting methods in loose labor markets. Of course, with a large volume of applications, firms may screen applicants intensively using tools designed to uncover desired skills (Manwaring and Wood 1984). When a firm has few applications, such intensive screening is not necessary since the firm has relatively few choices of job candidates.

This chapter uses the BALS data from employers to examine how firms recruit and screen workers for low-skilled positions. It addresses three propositions about firms' recruiting and screening of workers in low-skilled positions. It also uses BALS data from households to examine a fourth proposition, this one about individuals' behavior in applying for low-skilled jobs. If skills are truly an integral part of low-skilled jobs and not just used as screens for workers, we would expect firms' recruiting and screening methods to do three things:

1) vary with firm size,

2) relate to firms' stated needs for skills, and

3) vary in different types of labor markets.

If employers adapt recruiting methods and screens to the skills needed in the low-skilled position, we would expect low-skilled individuals with relatively high levels of skills (compared to other low-skilled individuals) to adapt job search methods to match the recruiting and screening by firms in order to maximize their success in finding employment.[5] Because low-skilled jobs requiring skills that are in relatively short supply pay increased wages (Chapter 3), the more-skilled individuals applying for low-skilled jobs have a higher probability of wage gains from using more-extensive job search methods than do lesser-skilled individuals, since the additional cost of extensively searching might uncover positions with higher wages. The more-skilled individuals seeking low-skilled positions would therefore engage in more sophisticated, costly job search methods, such as seeking out information about firms and positions before applying (Kahn and Low 1988), through either networking (Granovetter 1995) or the Internet (Kuhn and Skuterud 2000). If this is the case, the job search behavior of individuals wanting low-skilled positions will vary with their skill level.

The BALS data provide a unique opportunity to examine the hiring processes for workers in low-skilled positions from both the demand and the supply side of the market, and to test these four propositions. Firms were asked how they advertised for a low-skilled position (i.e., what their recruiting methods were) and the factors that affected their hiring decision (i.e., what their screening methods were). We use a factor analysis to distill the patterns in firms' recruiting and screening strategies. The factor analysis of recruiting methods uncovered three distinct patterns in recruiting: mass marketing, networking, and miscellaneous.[6] Firms engaging in mass marketing typically use job bulletins, job fairs, state agencies, schools and colleges, telephone job lines, and television and radio to announce positions. Firms using networking to locate potential workers rely on referrals or walk-ins and on verbal networking to advertise positions. Firms relying on miscellaneous means use temporary staffing agencies and newspapers to recruit. The factor analysis of screening practices uncovered four categories of screening: work experience, direct evidence, physical abilities, and references. Firms that use work experience to screen workers look at the applicant's history of employment, unemployment, and job experience. Firms that use direct evidence require a medical exam, tests, fingerprinting, and specific certificates. Firms that look for evidence of physical capabilities place requirements on physical ability and also require a drug test. The fourth category of screening requires work references.

We use the results of our factor analysis to classify a firm's recruiting and screening methods and to juxtapose the firm's methods with methods potential workers use. We also use the factor scores from each analysis to show the correlation between firms' recruiting and screening methods and the skills required in low-skilled positions.

FIRMS' RECRUITING AND SCREENING OF WORKERS VARIES WITH FIRM SIZE

The BALS data suggest that firms with low-skilled positions use a wide variety of recruiting and screening tools when searching for and hiring workers (Table 4.1). The vast majority of firms of all sizes—well over 85 percent—rely on networks to recruit applicants. The heavy reliance on referrals or verbal networking provides strong evidence of the potential of Granovetter's (1995) "strength of weak ties" factor in the job search, as firms may use existing workers as a low-cost way of informing potential applicants about a job opening.

Recruiting methods (other than networking) vary with the size of the firm; large firms are more likely than small firms to augment networks through mass marketing (Table 4.1). Over 60 percent of large firms, but only about 30 percent of small firms, post their job openings on the Internet. About half of all large firms, but only about one-fourth of small firms, use state employment agencies, job bulletins, and job fairs to recruit workers. About a fourth of all firms, irrespective of size, use temporary staffing agencies to recruit workers, and about two-thirds use newspapers to announce openings.

Perhaps because large firms use more extensive methods to recruit applicants, they use a greater number of screens than do small firms (Table 4.1). Even though over half of the small firms use work experience as a way of screening applicants, an even greater proportion—nearly three-quarters—of the large firms look at an applicant's work history. Large firms are more than twice as likely as small firms to use direct evidence when screening applicants, as nearly 33 percent require medical exams, nearly 40 percent require tests, and nearly 50 percent require drug tests.

One potential reason for different search methods across firm sizes is that large firms require more skills in their low-skilled positions. We examine for this possibility using the factor scores that were developed in Chapter 2 as measures of skill sets (Table 4.2). Factor scores would hover around zero in stratified analysis without skill differences across firm sizes, and would be above zero when firm size is positively correlated with skills. The analysis shows that small and large firms have higher skill needs than medium-sized firms. In fact, factor scores are

Table 4.1 Percentage of Low-Skilled Workers Affected by Recruiting and Screening Methods, by Firm Size

	Total	Small	Medium	Large
Recruiting methods				
Networking				
Referrals or walk-ins	87.4	85.4	89.2	88.3
Verbal networking	81.7	79.9	86.2	79.3
Mass market				
Hire from within	48.1	45.7	44.6	55.9
Web posting	44.9	32.3	46.9**	61.3**
Schools or colleges	41.5	40.9	34.6	50.5
State employment agency	33.3	22.6	33.1**	49.5**
Job bulletins	30.4	29.3	21.5	42.3**
Job fair	29.1	15.2	25.4**	54.1**
Phone job line	13.1	5.5	9.2	28.8**
TV/radio	8.1	3.7	5.4	18.0**
Miscellaneous				
Staffing services or temp agencies	23.0	19.6	24.6	26.1
Newspaper	65.4	65.8	65.4	64.9
Screening methods				
Work experience				
No long period of unemployment in the past	65.7	59.8	68.0	71.8**
No recent work history	61.8	58.5	65.9	62.0
Only short-term job experience	61.2	53.7	65.6**	67.3**
Direct evidence				
Medical exam	23.1	14.0	26.6**	32.7**
Tests	23.3	13.4	22.7**	39.1**
Fingerprinting	17.4	13.4	14.8	26.4
Any specific certifications	5.5	4.3	3.9	9.1
Physical				
Requirements on physical ability	54.7	51.2	56.3	58.2
Drug test	36.8	23.2	44.5**	48.2**
References				
Required for employment	81.3	78.7	83.6	82.7
N	405	164	130	111

NOTE: Data for firms are from the BALS Employer Survey. Numbers represent the percentage in each category. Small firms have from 1 to 49 employees. Medium firms have between 100 and 249 employees. Large firms have over 300 employees. There are gaps between the size categories to create a distinct difference between a small and a medium or a medium and a large firm. **indicates statistical significance ($p \leq 0.05$) between small and other-sized firms, as determined by a t-test.
SOURCE: HIRE (2006).

Table 4.2 Factor Analysis of Skills Required, by Firm Size

	Small	Medium	Large
New basic skill sets			
English skills			
Simple	−0.005	−0.066	0.085[a]
Complex	0.103[a]	−0.201	0.085[a]
Math			
Applied	0.213[a]	−0.258	−0.013
Algebra	−0.017	−0.138	0.188[a]
Measurement	0.027[a]	−0.030	−0.004
Problem-solving			
Prioritization	0.021[a]	−0.116	0.106[a]
Evaluation	0.180[a]	−0.192	−0.042
Leadership	0.122[a]	−0.100	−0.064
Communication			
Customers	0.219[a]	−0.268	−0.010
Coworkers	−0.046	−0.002	0.071[a]
Computer software			
Productivity enhancers	0.006	−0.067	0.071[a]
Multimedia	0.042[a]	0.061[a]	−0.135
Financial	0.070[a]	−0.014	−0.088
Job equipment skill sets			
Office	0.080[a]	−0.193	0.109[a]
Production	−0.179	0.170[a]	0.066[a]
N	163	130	111

NOTE: Data are from the BALS Employer Survey. Numbers are mean factor scores from the factor analysis of skills. Small firms have from 1 to 49 employees, medium firms have between 100 and 249 employees, and large firms have more than 300 employees. There are gaps between the size categories to create a distinct difference between a small and a medium or a medium and a large firm.
[a] Indicates relatively large, positive factor scores across firm sizes.
SOURCE: HIRE (2006).

negative in medium-sized firms in all but multimedia and production skills (suggesting that firms requiring relatively high levels of these skills may be of medium size). Small firms may require greater skill levels from their workers in low-skilled positions if fewer workers must cover a greater variety of job duties. Large firms may require greater skills to decrease the costs of monitoring work in a bureaucracy with large numbers of workers. For whatever reason, the relatively higher level of skills in small and large firms, as compared to medium-sized firms, suggests that differences in recruiting are not created by different skill needs.

If skill differences do not account for the more extensive recruiting and screening done by large firms, what does? One possibility is that large firms are better able than small firms to bear the additional expenses incurred from more extensive recruiting and screening of applicants. Size alone might afford large firms the opportunity to engage in a search for needed skills even if the needs for skills were the same as (or lower than) those needed by smaller firms.

FIRMS' RECRUITING AND SCREENING METHODS ARE RELATED TO SKILLS

Do firms' recruiting and screening of workers in low-skilled positions vary with needed skills as well as with firm size? The correlations between our measures of skill sets and recruiting and screening methods (Table 4.3) suggest that firms tailor recruiting and screening methods to the type of skills needed in the low-skilled positions. Firms use mass marketing (which would generate a large number of applicants) to recruit for English, customer and coworker communication, prioritizing and evaluation, math, productivity-enhancing software, and office equipment skills. This suggests that more extensive recruiting is done when firms require skills in low-skilled positions. Networking methods are not correlated with skills, and other recruiting methods ("miscellaneous") are positively correlated with simple English, algebra, productivity-enhancing, and production equipment skills. Results therefore suggest that firms requiring skills in a low-skilled position adopt more extensive recruiting methods to locate workers with the needed skills.

Screening methods also correlate with skill requirements (Table 4.3). Correlations suggest that firms adopt screens that are used to find appropriately skilled workers. Firms with jobs requiring English communication, productivity-enhancing software, and office equipment skills use direct evidence to screen for workers, as might be expected since each of these skill sets may be observable prior to hire. Positions using these skills, and positions requiring math, do not use physical requirements as screens, while positions requiring mechanical and large motor skills do. Firms use references when screening for all skills except large motor abilities.

Our analysis also suggests that recruiting and screening methods are correlated. Firms that use mass marketing in recruiting also use direct evidence as screens, while firms that rely on networking or on temp staffing and newspapers do not. These pairings seem logical given the need for information about relatively unknown applicants obtained through mass marketing. In contrast, firms using referrals and temporary staffing to generate applicants have information about individuals in their pool and therefore may not need direct evidence in screening. Not surprisingly, firms requiring work experience use work references as screens.

FIRMS MODIFY RECRUITING AND SCREENING METHODS WITH LABOR MARKET CONDITIONS

Since firms with low-skilled positions develop recruiting and screening tools to attract workers with needed skills, we would expect the composition of their tools to change between tight and loose labor markets, as fewer recruiting tools are needed to generate a large pool of applicants during a loose labor market. BALS data support this expectation and show that firms adopt less extensive recruiting methods when hiring in loose labor markets (Table 4.4). Firms are more likely to use newspapers, job bulletins, and community organizations in tight labor markets and are more likely to simply post a sign in the window when unemployment rates are high. Firms also increase the screens used during loose labor markets, suggesting they might be sifting through a greater number of applicants to find appropriate skill matches. As

Table 4.3 Correlation between Skills and Recruiting and Screening Methods

	Recruiting methods				Screening methods		
	Mass market	Networking	Misc.	Work experience	Direct evidence	Physical abilities	References
O*NET skills (with BALS data)							
New basics							
Communication and problem-solving	0.183****	0.016	0.022	0.058	0.193****	−0.242****	−0.022
Math	0.066	−0.046	0.043	−0.022	−0.097*	−0.191****	0.087*
Mechanical and physical							
Assembly	−0.056	0.019	−0.006	−0.002	0.004	0.082	−0.038
Mechanical	−0.084*	0.001	0.049	0.044	−0.003	0.252****	−0.072
Large motor	−0.161****	0.084*	−0.104**	−0.025	−0.049	0.353****	−0.129**
Small motor	−0.111**	0.063	−0.019	−0.008	−0.110**	0.013	−0.061
BALS skills							
New basic skill sets							
English							
Simple English	0.271****	0.023	0.149***	0.151**	0.193****	0.003	0.131***
Complex English	0.218****	0.007	0.063	0.205***	0.163****	−0.221****	0.067
Math							
Applied math	0.080	−0.046	−0.005	0.037	−0.058	−0.198****	0.055
Algebra	0.178****	−0.067	0.168****	0.166****	0.082	−0.039	0.104**
Measurement	0.134***	0.011	0.053	0.139***	0.073	0.135***	0.029
Problem-solving							
Prioritization	0.135***	0.040	0.048	0.163***	0.073	−0.023	0.118**

Evaluation	0.159***	−0.024	0.045	0.117**	0.002	−0.127**	−0.073
Leadership	−0.010	0.026	0.016	0.087*	0.045	0.069	0.094*
Communication							
Customers	0.154***	0.022	−0.049	0.037	0.028	−0.277****	0.087****
Coworkers	0.179****	0.031	0.069	0.046	0.111**	0.036	0.137***
Computer software							
Productivity enhancers	0.164****	−0.021	0.099**	0.122**	0.122**	−0.254****	0.167****
Multimedia	0.134	0.036	0.033	−0.041	−0.050	−0.099*	0.018
Financial	0.010	−0.027	−0.028	0.040	−0.125**	−0.154***	0.021
Job equipment skill sets							
Office	0.195****	−0.072	0.085	0.141***	0.112**	−0.284****	0.174****
Production	−0.013	−0.019	0.120**	0.112**	0.027	0.302****	−0.048
Screening methods							
Direct evidence	0.357****	−0.099**	−0.130***	0.082			
Physical abilities	0.008	0.005	0.045	0.061			
References	−0.027	0.039	0.094	0.148***			
N	400	400	400	395	395	395	395

NOTE: Data are from the BALS Employer Survey. Numbers are the Pearson correlation coefficients (ρ) between the factor scores of recruiting or screening methods and the factor score of skill sets. Asterisks indicate that ρ is statistically significant from 0 (**** $p \leq 0.001$, *** $p \leq 0.01$, ** $p \leq 0.05$, * $p \leq 0.10$). N varies slightly with item-specific nonresponse. Blank = not applicable.
SOURCE: HIRE (2006).

Table 4.4 Percentage of Low-Skilled Workers Affected by Recruiting and Screening Methods, by Type of Labor Market

	Tight	Medium	Loose
Recruiting methods			
Mass market			
Hire from within	55.1	23.4**	52.6
Web posting	48.3	45.5	40.8
Schools or colleges	49.4	28.6**	38.8
State employment agency	34.7	18.2**	39.5
Job bulletins	44.3	10.4**	24.3
Job fair	30.1	29.9	27.6
Phone job line	17.0	1.3**	14.5
TV/radio	10.8	3.9**	7.2
Networking			
Referrals or walk-ins	84.7	89.6	89.5
Verbal networking	80.7	88.3	79.6
Miscellaneous			
Newspaper	71.0	70.1	56.6
Staffing services or temp agencies	29.1	9.1**	23.0
Screening methods			
Work experience			
No long period of unemployment in the past	66.1	63.6	66.2
No recent work history	61.3	63.6	61.6
Only short-term job experience	57.8	54.5	69.9**
Direct evidence			
Medical exam	19.5	20.8	28.5
Tests	19.5	18.2	30.5**
Fingerprinting	16.1	13.0	21.2
Any specific certifications	5.7	3.9	6.0
Physical			
Requirements on physical ability	46.6	66.2	58.3
Drug test	25.3	46.7**	45.0
References			
Required for employment	78.2	93.5**	78.8
N	176	77	152

NOTE: Data are from the BALS Employer Survey. Numbers represent the percentage in each category. A tight labor market is one with a county-level unemployment rate between 2.2 and 4.2. A medium labor market has an unemployment rate between 4.7 and 5.9, and a loose labor market has an unemployment rate between 7.0 and 8.3. **indicates statistical significance ($p \leq 0.05$) between tight and other labor markets as determined by t-tests. N varies slightly with item-specific nonresponse.
SOURCE: HIRE (2006).

unemployment increases, more firms require drug tests, refuse to hire felons, increase the age restrictions, and are less likely to substitute education for work experience, suggesting that they raise hiring standards when labor is plentiful.[7]

MORE-SKILLED INDIVIDUALS USE MORE SOPHISTICATED JOB SEARCH METHODS FOR LOW-SKILLED POSITIONS

Because firms adapt recruiting and screening methods to obtain skills needed (and to reward needed skills in short supply), we expect that the more highly skilled individuals applying for low-skilled jobs will engage in more extensive job searches because they may receive increased wages as a result. BALS data support this proposition. Because work experience and education reflect individuals' level of skills (Table 4.5),[8] we can use them to approximate skill levels, as many employers do. In this analysis, we see that individuals either with some college or with work experience are almost four times more likely than individuals with no work experience and only a high school education to search for jobs using the Internet, and countless times more likely to go to job fairs and use telephone job lines (Table 4.6). They are less likely than the lower-skilled individuals to rely on informal job search methods such as television or radio and friends.[9]

SUMMARY AND CONCLUSIONS

The BALS data present a picture of firms' recruiting and screening of workers for low-skilled positions that is consistent with general search models. Firms adapt and coordinate recruiting and screening methods to obtain workers with the skills required in a low-skilled job. Individuals have adapted the job search to firms' behavior. The more skilled of the low-skilled individuals, who can reap benefits (increased wages) from matching their skills with the job, use more sophisticated and costly job search methods than lower-skilled individuals. As a result, the more skilled may be more likely to find employment in larger

Table 4.5 Skills, Work Experience, and Education: Supply Side

	Work experience		Education		
	No long-term work experience	Long-term stable work experience	High school dropout	High school graduate	College
New basic skill sets					
English					
Simple English	2.54	3.73**	2.16	3.14**	4.00**
Complex English	0.93	1.66**	0.65	1.23**	1.87**
Math					
Applied math	1.84	2.37**	1.60	2.07**	2.53**
Algebra	1.50	2.34**	0.98	1.83**	2.69**
Measurement	1.24	1.59**	1.22	1.41**	1.63**
Problem-solving					
Prioritization	2.11	2.91**	1.94	2.66**	2.97**
Evaluation	1.32	2.03**	1.27	1.84**	2.03**
Leadership	2.41	3.21**	2.37	3.01**	3.19**
Communication					
Customers	2.06	3.34**	1.87	2.94**	3.40**
Coworkers	1.39	2.22**	1.31	1.91**	2.27**
Computer software					
Productivity enhancers	1.40	2.13**	0.68	1.46**	2.67**
Multimedia	0.35	0.54**	0.14	0.42**	0.66**
Financial	0.05	0.15**	0.02	0.11	0.16**

Job equipment skill sets					
Office equipment	2.25	3.32**	1.79	2.86**	3.57**
Production equipment	0.34	0.57**	0.43	0.51	0.52
N	204	468	141	189	342

NOTE: Data are from the BALS Household Survey. Numbers represent average number of skills held in each set. **indicates statistical significance ($p \leq 0.05$) between work experience categories, or between high school dropouts and other education levels, as determined by a t-test. N varies slightly with item-specific nonresponse.

SOURCE: HIRE (2006).

Table 4.6 Job-Seeking by Low-Skilled Individuals

Methods used to find job	Job seekers		
	Total	Low skill	Medium skill
Mass market			
Internet	38.9	11.4	42.0**
School/college	3.8	2.9	2.0
One-Stop	1.5	0.0	0.0
Job bulletins	4.6	5.7	4.0
Job fair	4.6	0.0	8.0**
Telephone job line	3.8	0.0	4.0**
TV/radio	7.6	14.3	4.0**
Networking			
Friend/referral	32.1	40.0	22.0**
Church	1.5	2.9	2.0
Walk-in	27.5	40.0	26.0**
Miscellaneous			
Newspaper	58.0	54.3	62.0
Staffing/temp services	16.0	14.3	24.0**
N	131	35	50

NOTE: Data are from the BALS Household Survey. "Low skill" consists of individuals with no more than a high school education *and* no more than one year of work experience. "Medium skill" consists of individuals with no more than a high school education *or* no more than one year of work experience. **indicates a statistically significant ($p \leq 0.05$) difference between low- and medium-skilled workers as determined by a t-test. N varies slightly with item-specific nonresponse.
SOURCE: HIRE (2006).

firms, which, as Chapter 3 showed, pay higher wages, and in occupations that pay increased wages for skills.

Because firms formulate recruiting and screening strategies to acquire workers with needed skills in low-skilled positions, behavioral differences emerge in different-sized firms and between tight and loose labor markets. Large firms use extensive search methods for low-skilled positions more frequently than small firms, even though both sizes of firms require relatively high levels of skills (as compared to medium-sized firms). Larger firms use a wider variety of screening methods than smaller firms, too. Firms also adapt recruiting and screening methods to changes in the supply of labor. As unemployment rates rise, firms use less extensive recruiting methods, as would be expected with greater numbers of applicants. However, they also adopt more intensive screening methods as they sift through the greater number of applicants.

Notes

1. Rosenbaum (2001) notes that, rather than rely on recommendations, employers use interviews (for example) to gather clues about workers' skills by noting applicants' demeanor, speaking style, eye contact, appearance, etc., simply because they "trust their gut." Of course, another interpretation of such behavior is that employers are invoking racial and ethnic biases in hiring (Neckerman and Kirschenman 1991; Avery and Faley 1988).
2. Screens such as education or work experience may not be valued for the human capital they build, but for their correlation with a detailed set of skills required in the job. For example, employers may require work experience because low-skilled individuals with work experience are more likely to be reliable, show up on time, etc., than individuals without work experience. Such employers may not value work experience for the skills it imparts.
3. For example, it may be easier to communicate (and to garner sympathy for one's view) that "high school graduates can't write" than to communicate that "my intake receptionists can't accurately record the needs of clients." Even if individuals that can "write" are more likely to accurately record clients' needs than those that "can't write," the two concerns have very different implications for firms' recruiting and screening methods. The requirement of using writing on the job suggests that employers will screen applicants based on writing and might use such tools as grades in English courses in hiring. Decoding intake information accurately suggests that employers might use a high school diploma as an initial screening device (since it is correlated with writing ability) but will hire applicants based on their ability to accurately record information, as uncovered with screening tools (e.g., requiring a test asking applicants to summarize information from an audiotape), a logic supported by case study research (Bils 1988, 1999).
4. Firms will also bear the costs of an extensive search if high training costs exist. Because low-skilled positions do not require extensive training, we do not discuss these implications here.
5. Each search strategy is pursued until its marginal cost equals its marginal benefit (Benhabib and Bull 1983; Osberg 1993).
6. Full results of the factor analysis are available from the author.
7. In results not shown here but available from the author, BALS data show that change is more likely for firms that move from tight to loose labor markets than for firms that stay in loose labor markets. Firms moving from a tight to a loose labor market were more likely than firms staying in a loose labor market to in-

crease employment duties, to increase work experience required for employment, to advance employees to the next level, and to increase the requirements needed for employment (and to go out of business!).

8. Use of education and work experience as proxies for skills seems appropriate since individuals with long-term work experience report significantly higher levels of all skill sets than individuals without such experience, and high school graduates and individuals with some college report higher levels of all skill sets than high school dropouts.

9. We do not examine job search behavior of high-skilled individuals—those with college degrees and extensive work experience—because they are unlikely to be searching for a low-skilled position.

5
Skills, Promotions, and Low-Skilled Positions

I'm the type of person that does not give up very easily. Even if it is a challenge, even if I'm struggling with something and I know it is going to be very difficult for me to accomplish, I make it personal. I'll do anything it takes to accomplish my goals.
—A low-wage worker

Analysis in the preceding chapters suggests that firms recruit, screen, require, and pay for specific skills when they hire workers in low-skilled positions. These findings raise the possibility that firms might use promotional opportunities to retain workers in low-skilled jobs with needed skills, in contrast to the dead-end nature of jobs predicted by our conventional model.

Promotions are one way firms provide incentives for workers to develop and use their skills effectively and to remain with the firm: their presence causes workers to invest in human capital, reduce shirking on the job, and increase tenure with the firm (Gibbons and Waldman 1999a,b; Lazear and Rosen 1981; Rosen 1986). Phrased somewhat differently, workers respond to the incentives of increased wages or the status of moving up the job ladder by gaining needed skills, working hard, and staying with the firm. Firms can benefit greatly from these actions, as skill investments and work effort increase workers' capacity to use skills and also increase their productivity on the job. Of course, these considerations become irrelevant if workers are homogeneous and easily replaced. It is the need for skills, in the presence of hiring costs, that provides the incentive for firms to structure promotional opportunities and to increase earnings to reward workers with needed skills for staying with the firm (Andersson, Holzer, and Lane 2005; Baron, Davis-Blake, and Bielby 1986; Carmichael 1983).

The manner in which firms structure the incentives—promotions and wage increases—is critical (Baker, Jensen, and Murphy 1988), even though a close relationship exists between the two.[1] If firms structure an internal labor market with wage increases but no change in job duties, workers have an incentive only to remain with the firm and not to invest in building (or retaining) skills. If firms structure an internal labor market with promotional opportunities but no wage gains, only status-seeking workers will remain with the firm. If firms structure an internal labor market with promotions that require a change in job duties and carry wage increases, workers will invest in skills and stay with the firm (Prendergast 1993).

Job hierarchies that require workers to expand skills to move up may provide entry-level workers with an incentive to invest in the skills needed to advance (unless they bring the needed skills to the entry-level job—i.e., are overqualified for the entry-level position), if the expansion of duties is properly structured. Few workers would invest in building a completely new set of skills unless the wage increase upon promotion was large.[2] As a result, few firms will structure such an internal labor market, as the risk is great of not generating a pool of qualified workers for the next job in the hierarchy. Instead, firms will structure internal labor markets so that the skills required after a promotion relate to and expand upon the position below it (Pergamit and Veum 1999). Firms can, of course, increase the probability of obtaining a pool of candidates that can move through the internal labor market if they search for entry-level workers with the skills for the position above the entry-level job (Rosenbaum 2001).

By hiring with the next position in mind, firms have a chance to build a pipeline of qualified workers for the internal labor market. They also increase the probability that their entry-level workers will develop and use skills effectively, because they possess skills close to those required for the promotion. Phrased somewhat differently, entry-level workers with skills beyond entry level will have a strong incentive to invest in the few new skills needed to gain the promotion because, as long as they perform effectively in the initial job, they can move quickly up the job ladder. Hiring workers with skills far below those needed in the next job in the hierarchy reduces the skill-development incentives of the promotion because a worker's investment must be great to move up the job ladder.

We examine promotional opportunities from the entry-level, low-skilled position to determine their existence and structure. If firms require skills in a low-skilled job and, implicitly, the job above it, we would expect them to structure internal labor markets so that duties increase and require a modest expansion in skills in the job above entry level. Such a structure provides workers in low-skilled jobs with an incentive to invest in needed skills and to remain with the firm. We might also expect firms to hire entry-level workers with the skills close to those needed in the position above entry so as to ensure a flow of appropriately skilled applicants into the internal labor market. We define a promotional opportunity as one in which a position above the entry-level job exists that is attainable without the worker increasing education. The BALS Employer Survey asked employers whether such a position exists, its job title, its duties, and the skills used in it. BALS information therefore enables us to examine the promotional opportunities afforded to workers in entry-level, low-skilled jobs and to describe their structure in terms of skill requirements.

If firms structure promotional opportunities to provide incentives for skill retention and development in workers in entry-level, low-skilled positions, we would expect to see four things:

1) positions above the entry level with expanded duties (to provide incentives for skill development),

2) a correlation between skills required in the entry-level position and those required in the position above it (to structure appropriately the skill development incentives),

3) workers at entry level with qualifications above those set for the entry-level position (to ensure a pipeline of appropriately skilled workers for the internal labor market), and

4) skills with a high relative demand having an increased probability of a promotional opportunity from the entry-level job (to provide workers that have relatively scarce skills with an incentive to remain with the firm).

PROMOTIONAL OPPORTUNITIES WITH EXPANDED DUTIES EXIST

Despite the presumed dead-end nature of low-skilled positions, the BALS data suggest that the vast majority have advancement potential (Table 5.1), and that most of these present a variety of paths for advancement (Table A.6). Promotional opportunities exist within the firm in 81.7 percent of the low-skilled positions in BALS firms. If workers in low-skilled positions wish to move to another firm, advancement potential is even more likely, as 94 percent of the job titles have a position above entry level to which the worker can advance without getting more education (Table A.6).

The probability of having a promotional opportunity from the entry-level, low-skilled job varies depending on the entry-level occupation (Table 5.1). While all of the entry-level job titles in business and financial operations, community and social services, health care practitioner and technical, and the military have promotional opportunities, only half of the positions in farming, fishing, and forestry have advancement potential unless workers increase their education.

Of primary interest is the promotional potential from the six occupational groups housing the majority of entry-level, low-skilled positions, since advancement from these occupations may typify the potential of the entry-level worker in a low-skilled position to move into an internal labor market. Over 80 percent of the office and administrative support positions—which house nearly half of all entry-level, low-skilled positions in the BALS labor market—have promotional opportunities, as do 88 percent of the transportation positions, 86 percent of the production positions, 81 percent of the maintenance positions, 80 percent of the sales positions, and 75 percent of the food preparation and serving positions. These data suggest that promotional opportunities are fairly ubiquitous for workers in entry-level, low-skilled positions, despite the portrayal of such positions as dead-end.

BALS data also suggest that promotional opportunities require expanded duties, with advancement moving the worker into a position of more responsibility. The modal job title of the position above entry level is a lead, supervisor, or manager (Table A.6). Over half (51.9 percent) of the promotional opportunities in sales are for a lead, supervisor,

Table 5.1 Differences in Promotional Opportunities by Occupation

2-Digit SOC	Occupational category	% with next position	n
13	Business and financial operations	100.0	2
21	Community and social services	100.0	3
29	Health care practitioner and technical	100.0	11
55	Military	100.0	1
33	Protective service	90.9	43
39	Personal care and service	90.0	10
53	Transportation and material moving	88.1	42
31	Health care support	87.5	8
51	Production	86.0	43
49	Installation, maintenance, and repair	83.3	12
25	Education, training, and library	81.8	11
37	Building and grounds cleaning and maintenance	81.3	32
43	Office and administrative support	81.2	133
41	Sales and related	80.0	50
35	Food preparation and serving related	75.0	32
47	Construction and extraction	71.4	7
27	Art, design, entertainment, sports, and media	66.7	3
45	Farming, fishing, and forestry	50.0	4
Average		81.7	
N			405

NOTE: Numbers represent the percentage of jobs in each two-digit standard occupational classification (SOC) having a position above entry level that the worker can obtain without further education. Blank = not applicable.
SOURCE: BALS Employer Survey (HIRE 2006).

or manager position, as are 32 percent of the opportunities in building and grounds maintenance, 36 percent of the opportunities in food, about 30 percent of the opportunities in production and transportation, and 18 percent of the opportunities in office and administrative support. Firms may also take a position that would be considered entry-level at some firms and structure it as a second-level position, while keeping the job title the same. Such cases would entail promotion and expanded responsibilities, despite the fact that the position doesn't carry the title of lead, supervisor, or manager. Nearly half (49.1 percent) of the jobs held after a promotion from office and administrative support positions have the same job title as entry-level positions, as do about 57 percent of jobs held after promotion in maintenance, 44 percent of the jobs in food preparation, and about 20 percent of the jobs in production and transportation.

We explicitly examine whether skill usage increases between the entry-level position and the one above it by comparing skills in each (Table 5.2). We see that *all* English, math, problem-solving, and computer software (except multimedia authoring) skills are required at a significantly higher rate in the position above entry level. Only 37.5 percent of the communication skills are required at a higher rate above entry level, with all increases coming in the area of customer service. Job equipment skills increasingly are required in the position above entry level, with the exception of using production machinery and heavy equipment.

The high level and increased use of English and problem-solving skills in the position above entry suggest the direction that promotions might take the worker after the entry-level, low-skilled position. In fact, virtually all promotional opportunities require English skills, and most require problem-solving skills (Table 5.2). Between 80 and 90 percent of positions above entry level require filling out forms, recording information, writing simple sentences, reading written instructions, and reading forms, memos, and letters. Over 57 percent require the worker to organize information into a brief written report, and about 45 percent require the worker to write letters using correct structure and sentence style and to proofread—nearly double the percentage of entry-level jobs using these skills.

The vast majority of low-skilled jobs above entry level also require problem-solving skills. Over 80 percent require the worker to identify work-related problems and prioritize tasks, a 20 percent increase over the use of these skills in entry-level jobs. Over 70 percent of jobs above entry require workers to identify potential solutions to problems, gather information, identify barriers to solutions, collaboratively problem-solve, and sort and categorize information. Over 60 percent require workers to make decisions independently, implement solutions to problems, and evaluate results. Problem-solving skills show a sharp growth in use: between a 48 and a 130 percent increase for most jobs above entry. Leadership-oriented problem-solving has a 222 percent increase, and nearly half the jobs above entry use these skills. The relatively large increase in problem-solving skill use suggests that the job after promotion carries more responsibility than the entry-level job.

Math and computer software skills also witness large percentage increases in use in the job above entry, in part because they are used far less than English and problem-solving skills in the entry-level job. Entry-level workers may be able to get low-skilled jobs without these skills, but they may not be able to advance unless they can use math and computer software.

SKILLS IN THE ENTRY-LEVEL POSITION ARE CORRELATED WITH SKILLS IN THE NEXT POSITION

A cursory view of job titles and skill needs in the low-skilled positions above entry suggests that promotional opportunities are structured to expand upon skills used in the entry-level job, a proposition we examine more closely using Pearson correlation coefficients and a canonical correlation to compare skill usage in the entry-level, low-skilled job and the position above it. As a first step in this analysis, we determine the skill sets used in the job above entry level. Our factor analysis of the 53 skills potentially used in the job above entry finds 13 skill sets, a reduction from the 15 skill sets used in the entry-level position.[3] Applied math and algebra skill sets combine to form a single math set in the position above entry level, and the use of financial software is no longer a discernible skill set.[4]

When we examine the correlation between skill sets used in the entry-level job and those used in the position above it using Pearson correlations (Table 5.3), we see a relatively high correlation. Correlations are strongest between the same skill sets (i.e., the correlation is higher along the diagonal than off the diagonal). This pattern of correlation suggests that skill sets used in the entry-level position are also used in the position above it.

Table 5.2 Skills Required in the Entry-Level Job and Next Position

Skill	Entry-level position	Next position	% change
English			
Read written instructions, safety warnings, labels (product or shipping), invoices/work orders, logs and journals	78.3	85.4**	9.1
Write simple sentences, short notes, and simple memos	77.6	87.2**	12.4
Fill out forms, record data and time on log or chart	74.1	89.1**	20.2
Read manuals, computer printouts, contracts, and agreements	73.8	86.6**	17.3
Read forms, memos, and letters	67.6	82.1**	21.4
Write letters using correct structure and sentence style	24.2	45.9**	89.7
Proofread	23.4	45.3**	93.6
Organize information into a brief written report	22.9	57.8**	152.4
Math			
Use measurement instruments (e.g., ruler, scale)	44.9	57.3**	27.6
Use equipment such as a calculator, cash register, business machine	43.9	56.1**	27.8
Perform simple measurements (e.g., lengths, volumes)	41.6	54.9**	32.0
Solve simple equations	34.2	56.1**	64.0
Estimate or round off numbers	32.7	47.9**	46.5
Make change	30.7	37.8**	23.1
Use ratios, fractions, decimals, or percentages	27.4	46.0**	67.9
Compute or figure discounts, markups, or selling price	17.2	30.8**	79.1
Interpret data from graphs, tables, or charts	13.5	31.4**	132.6
Problem-solving			
Identify work-related problems	70.3	86.0**	22.3
Prioritize tasks	68.8	82.7**	20.2

Teamwork/collaborative problem-solving	63.3	74.2**	17.2
Gather information	62.6	78.7***	25.7
Identify potential solutions to problems	52.9	79.9***	51.0
Sort and categorize information	48.1	71.1***	47.8
Identify barriers to solutions	44.1	74.5***	68.9
Make decisions independently	35.2	65.3***	85.5
Implement solutions	31.7	62.9***	98.4
Evaluate results	26.9	61.7***	129.4
Leadership-oriented problem-solving	14.5	46.8**	222.8
Communication			
Interact with coworkers to accomplish a task	90.8	89.4	-1.5
Choose words and manner of expression appropriately at work	85.3	86.0	0.8
Be perceptive of verbal and nonverbal cues from others	81.5	84.5	3.7
Deal with customers	64.6	69.9	8.2
Make and receive business phone calls	49.4	61.7**	24.9
Explain products and services	47.6	61.4**	29.0
Handle complaints	47.4	63.8**	34.6
Sell a product or service to a customer	28.4	39.2**	38.0
Computer software			
Use word processing programs	27.4	43.0**	56.9
Use e-mail	23.2	38.4**	65.5
Use spreadsheet programs	20.4	36.9**	80.9
Use database software	17.2	28.0**	62.8
Use Internet browsers	16.0	24.7**	54.4
Use financial inventory software	3.0	7.0**	133.3

(continued)

Table 5.2 (continued)

Skill	Entry-level position	Next position	% change
Computer software			
Use graphics software	2.5	6.4**	156.0
Use Web page design/authoring	1.7	4.3**	152.9
Use desktop publishing programs	1.5	4.9**	226.7
Use multimedia authoring and editing software	1.0	1.8	80.0
Job equipment			
Use telephone systems	63.6	75.1**	18.1
Use copiers	44.9	59.3**	32.1
Use fax machines	42.1	56.5**	34.2
Use answering machines	37.9	52.9**	39.6
Use Windows or DOS-based computers	34.2	52.9**	54.7
Use production equipment	15.2	18.8	23.7
Use heavy equipment	12.0	14.3	19.2
N	401	329	

NOTE: **indicates statistical significance ($p \leq 0.05$) between the positions as determined by a t-test. Numbers represent the percentage in each category or the percentage change between entry level and position above. Employers were asked which skills employees in the entry-level position are expected to use and which skills the position above it uses.
SOURCE: BALS Employer Survey (HIRE 2006).

Table 5.3 Skill Set Correlations between Entry-Level Job and Next Position

Skill sets in entry-level position	Skill sets in next position												
	English		Math		Problem-Solving			Computer Software		Communication		Job Equipment	
	Simple English	Complex English	Math	Measurement	Prioritize	Evaluative	Leadership	Prod. enhance	Multimedia	Customer	Coworker	Office equip.	Prod. equip.
English													
Simple English	0.419[a,b]	0.418[a]	0.274	0.135	0.254	0.279	0.128	0.371	0.084	0.229	0.246	0.377	−0.131
Complex English	0.240	0.604[a,b]	0.340	0.141	0.225	0.266	0.131	0.428[a]	0.101	0.360	0.196	0.373	−0.221
Math													
Algebra	0.151	0.412[a]	0.527[a,b]	0.435[a]	0.131	0.269	0.131	0.392	0.205	0.215	0.070	0.315	0.039
Applied math	0.127	0.342	0.593[a,b]	0.091	0.169	0.248	0.155	0.315	0.100	0.456[a]	0.093	0.357	−0.144
Measurement	0.174	0.115	0.193	0.702[a,b]	0.239	0.171	0.237	0.017	0.007	0.081	0.195	0.054	0.260
Problem-solving													
Prioritization	0.209	0.402[a]	0.271	0.157	0.412[a,b]	0.320	0.313	0.340	0.038	0.232	0.178	0.339	−0.084
Evaluation	0.162	0.369	0.252	0.134	0.173	0.436[a,b]	0.120	0.163	0.185	0.299	0.178	0.184	−0.030
Leadership	0.119	0.167	0.155	0.098	0.194	0.134	0.507[a,b]	0.143	−0.142	0.117	0.133	0.212	0.098
Computer software													
Productivity enhance	0.115	0.447[a]	0.316	0.045	0.093	0.107	0.175	0.673[a,b]	0.250	0.211	0.087	0.443[a]	−0.210
Multimedia	0.029	0.105	0.073	−0.024	−0.034	0.081	0.020	0.083	0.603[a,b]	0.046	−0.065	0.046	−0.085
Financial	0.091	0.147	0.106	0.036	0.119	0.116	0.053	0.269	0.195	0.128	0.090	0.178	−0.086
Communication													
Customers	0.115	0.467[a]	0.433[a]	−0.048	0.146	0.355	0.178	0.383	0.049	0.629[a,b]	0.108	0.457[a]	−0.332
Coworkers	0.222	0.242	0.162	0.108	0.268	0.219	0.185	0.255	0.019	0.182	0.417[a,b]	0.282	−0.143
Job equipment													
Office equipment	0.194	0.577[a]	0.400[a]	−0.005	0.226	0.240	0.191	0.697[a]	0.204	0.375	0.148	0.661[a,b]	−0.279
Production machinery	0.074	−0.122	−0.038	0.262	−0.005	0.045	0.053	−0.190	0.002	−0.252	−0.061	−0.145	0.772[a,b]

NOTE: Numbers represent the Pearson correlation coefficients between the skill sets required in the entry-level job and those required in the position above entry level.

[a] Indicates correlations that exceed 0.4.

[b] Indicates the correlation between the skill set for the entry-level job and the same skill set for the position above i. The factor analysis of skills in the job above entry level produced a reduced number of sets from that of the entry-level job.

SOURCE: BALS Employer Survey (HIRE 2006).

All skill sets used in the entry-level job have a 0.4 correlation or better with the equivalent skill set in the position above it. Yet some skill sets used in the entry-level job have a high likelihood of skill expansion into other areas, as evidenced by correlation coefficients exceeding 0.4 in the off diagonal. If an entry-level job uses office equipment skills, the position above it may also use complex English, math, and productivity enhancers. If the entry-level job uses communication-with-customer skills, the position above it may also use complex English, math, and office equipment skills. An entry-level job using productivity-enhancing skills might require complex English in the job above it, and an entry-level job using algebra might require complex English and measurement in the job above entry. When this analysis is viewed in conjunction with the descriptive analysis presented in Table 5.2, it confirms the increasing use of English language skills in the position above entry level.

We can determine how many of the differences in skill use in the jobs above entry can be explained by the skill use in the entry-level job by using canonical correlation analysis. We use this analysis to determine 1) the proportion of variance in *skill sets* used in the position above entry level that can be explained by the skill sets used in the entry-level position, and 2) the proportion of variance in *individual skills* required in the position above entry level that can be explained by the individual skills required in the entry-level position. The former, more aggregate analysis, tells us how closely knit skill-set usage is between the entry-level position and the one above it, while the latter analysis tells us how interrelated individual skills are between the two positions.

Canonical correlation is a statistical tool grounded in the estimation of a canonical variable that is a linear combination of variables, in our case either the skill sets or individual skills in the entry-level position and those in the position above it. The canonical variable is estimated in such a way that the correlation between the skills or skill sets in each position is maximized.[5] Each canonical variable is uncorrelated with all other canonical variables of either set except for the one corresponding canonical variable developed from the opposite position. We use a canonical redundancy analysis to examine how well the skill sets and individual skills used in the position above entry level can be predicted from the skill sets and individual skills in the entry-level position.

Our canonical correlation analysis (Table 5.4) confirms our finding that skills used in the positions above entry level are, by and large, an expansion of the skills used in the entry-level jobs. Over 40 percent of the variance in the skill sets used in positions above entry level can be explained by the skill sets used in the entry-level positions. When we look at individual skills, we see a similar pattern for use of math, job equipment, and computer software skills: over 40 percent of the variance in their skill use in the position above entry can be explained by their use in the entry-level position. Communication skills in the entry-level job explain only about one-third of their use in the next job, and problem-solving and English skill use in the entry-level position explain only about one-quarter of their use in the position above entry. As we saw in the previous analysis (Table 5.2), both English and problem-solving skills are heavily used in jobs above entry.

Table 5.4 Percentage of Skills Used in the Position above Entry Explained by Entry-Level Skills: Canonical Correlation Analysis

Skill sets	% variance explained in skills in next position by skills in entry-level position
All skill sets	41.5
Individual skills	
Job equipment skills	44.9
Math skills	44.3
Computer software skills	41.0
Communication skills	31.3
English skills	25.8
Problem-solving skills	24.4

NOTE: Estimates are from seven different canonical correlation analyses: one using the factor score measures of skill sets, and six using the individual skill measures in each grouping. Numbers represent the percentage of standardized variance explained by the skill sets in the position above entry level, as determined by the canonical variables. In other words, the analysis explains what percentage of the skills in the job above entry level can be explained by the skill requirements in the entry-level position. For example, the 15 skill sets required in entry-level positions explain 41.5 percent of the variance in skill sets required in positions above entry level. The reading skills required in the entry-level positions explain 25.8 percent of the reading skills required in positions above entry level.

SOURCE: BALS Employer Survey (HIRE 2006).

SUCCESSFUL APPLICANTS HAVE ABOVE-MINIMUM QUALIFICATIONS

Because the promotional opportunities carry expanded job duties over the entry-level position, employers have an incentive to hire for the future by searching for entry-level workers with the skills needed in the position above entry level. If they can find such individuals, they will increase the probability that entry-level workers will have the skills to move up through the internal labor market. One manifestation of firms' hiring for the next position would be that the qualifications of successful applicants for the entry-level position would greatly exceed the minimum level posted. We see from Table 5.5 that this is the case. Stated requirements for workers in low-skilled positions are modest: over half of the jobs do not require a high school degree, nearly 60 percent require no work experience, and only about half require a high level of English proficiency. Incumbents filling low-skilled positions hold credentials that far exceed the advertised requirements, however. Almost 20 percent of the workers in entry-level, low-skilled jobs have some college (no degree), almost 30 percent have two or more years of work experience, and about 60 percent have a high level of English proficiency.

One explanation for the discrepancy between the stated requirements for education, work experience, and English in the jobs and the levels held by incumbents is an excess supply of workers. This is not the case in the BALS labor market, however, as close to 60 percent of the employers reported difficulties in getting qualified applicants, and a high relative demand exists for (simple) English skills. A more plausible explanation might be that employers are hiring entry-level workers with the next position in mind (Rosenbaum 2001).

Indeed, when we examine the education, work experience, and English requirements for the position above entry, we see that over half (50.9 percent) require a high school diploma or GED (with 6 percent requiring some vocational or technical education). About 10 percent require some college, and 3.4 percent require a bachelor's degree or higher. Nearly 30 percent require two or more years of work experience, and over 70 percent require the individual to speak, understand, and read English very well. These requirements align closely with the education,

Table 5.5 Human Capital Needed to Obtain, Succeed, and Advance

Human capital	Minimum required	Average workers	Position above entry
Education			
None	38.8		
Less than high school	14.0	18.1**	16.4**
High school graduate	43.5	60.1**	49.8
GED	2.5	1.6	1.1**
Vocational/technical	0.3	0.5	6.0**
College (no degree)	1.0	17.5**	10.4**
Associate degree	0.0	0.3	1.1**
Bachelor's degree	0.0	1.9**	3.0**
Graduate degree	0.0	0.0	0.4
Other (e.g., performance)	0.0	0.0	6.0**
Work experience			
None	59.8	12.3**	2.8**
Less than one year	20.0	24.5	9.4**
One year	15.3	16.2	10.8
Between one and two years	2.3	17.5**	17.1**
Two or more years	1.3	28.5**	28.3**
Preferred	0.3	0.0	0.4
Amount depends on skill	0.8	0.8	14.0**
Other (e.g., performance)	0.5	0.3	11.2**
English ability			
Speak very well	45.7	60.1**	72.1**
Understand very well	52.7	61.7**	74.4**
Read very well	50.1	59.7**	71.8**
N	405	405	405

NOTE: **indicates statistical significance ($p \leq 0.05$) exists between minimum required and other categories as determined by a t-test. N varies slightly with item-specific non-response. Numbers represent percentage in each category. Employers were asked to identify the minimum level of education, work experience, and English ability needed for job (i.e., advertised requirements), the level held by the average employee in the job, and the level needed to advance to the next position. Because education levels for incumbent workers and workers in the position above entry exceed "None," we use a blank space to illustrate nonapplicability of the category in these columns. Questions on moving up were not asked in San Francisco County.
SOURCE: BALS Employer Survey (HIRE 2006).

work experience, and English skills held by successful applicants. We note that while workers in entry-level, low-skilled positions will, by definition, gain work experience once hired, there is no guarantee that they will gain the needed academic and English language skills. Hiring entry-level workers with these skills ensures employers of a supply of workers to the position above entry when qualified applicants for low-skilled jobs are hard to come by.

SKILL REQUIREMENTS IN ENTRY-LEVEL JOBS DO NOT DETERMINE ADVANCEMENT POTENTIAL

Firms may have a greater incentive to build promotional ladders for workers whose skills are relatively scarce in the entry-level position because they want to retain workers with these relatively scarce skills. We test for this possibility using the general occupational wage equation presented in Chapter 3 and estimate whether or not the job has a position above entry:

$$(4.1) \quad Adv_j = \alpha_0^1 + Skills_j \alpha^1 + Inst_j \beta^1 + \gamma^1 LM + \varepsilon_1,$$

where

      Adv = advancement potential in the entry-level job as measured by a binary variable, with 1 indicating a promotional opportunity above the entry-level job (j),

and other variables are defined in Chapter 3 following Equation (3.1), page 64.

We find little support for this proposition, as shown in Table 5.6. Only entry-level positions using prioritization skills, which are in short supply in the BALS local labor market, have an increased probability ($p \leq 0.05$) of a promotional opportunity. Workers in entry-level, low-skilled positions using leadership skills may have an increased probability of having a promotional opportunity ($p \leq 0.10$), but these skills are relatively easy for the firm to obtain, which is inconsistent with the notion that firms would build promotional ladders to retain only those workers with skills in short supply.

Table 5.6 The Relationship between Skills and Occupational Wages: Odds Ratios

Skill sets	Level of demand	Promotional opportunity
New basic skill sets		
English		
Simple English	High D	1.279
Complex English	Low D	1.235
Math		
Applied math	Low D	0.854
Algebra	Low D	1.060
Measurement	Low D	0.985
Problem-solving		
Prioritization	High D	1.638**
Evaluation	Mixed D	0.862
Leadership	Low D	0.747*
Communication		
Customers	Mixed D	0.840
Coworkers	High D	1.160
Computer software		
Productivity enhancers	Mixed D	0.976
Multimedia software	Low D	1.549
Financial software	Low D	0.924
Job equipment skill sets		
Office equipment	Mixed D	0.823
Production equipment	Low D	1.412
Mean dependent variable		0.829
N		398

NOTE: ** $p \leq 0.05$; * $p \leq 0.10$. Numbers represent the odds ratios from a logit estimation. Estimation results for independent variables included in the model, other than skills, are not reported. See Table 3.6 in Chapter 3 for a more complete listing (excluding only county unemployment rate). Full results are available from the author. Blank = not applicable.

SOURCE: BALS Employer Survey (HIRE 2006).

SUMMARY AND CONCLUSIONS

Low-skilled jobs offer promotional opportunities from the entry-level position. In fact, over 80 percent of the BALS entry-level jobs have a position to which the worker can advance without increasing education. In general, firms structure job hierarchies from entry-level, low-skilled jobs by expanding the skills needed in the position above entry, as suggested by the modal job title upon promotion: lead, manager, or supervisor. Thus, the job a worker has after a promotion will require that worker to expand on the skills that were used in the entry-level job, especially English and problem-solving skills. The new job also may require the worker to gain math and computer software skills.

Employers may be maximizing the potential that entry-level workers will have the requisite skills to move up the promotional ladder by hiring workers that have at least some of the skills needed for the position above entry level. Successful applicants to the entry-level, low-skilled positions have qualifications that greatly exceed the minimum level posted; in fact, the level of skills of hirees approaches that of those needed in the next job in the hierarchy. BALS data suggest that employers structure a job hierarchy for workers in entry-level, low-skilled positions and that they attempt to build a pipeline of appropriately skilled workers to move through it. In other words, internal labor markets with promotional opportunities for workers in low-skilled jobs exist. The jobs of these workers are not necessarily dead-end.

Notes

1. Promotion accounts for about 15 percent of wage growth for the average full-time worker (McCue 1996), and wages are strongly related to job levels in a firm, despite modest within-job-level variations (Baker, Gibbs, and Holmstrom 1994).
2. We are assuming implicitly that job hierarchies in low-skilled jobs do not rely on such incentives as tournament structures, in which a few large wage payoffs are made to a cadre of workers making relatively large investments in skill building. It seems reasonable to assume that individuals who have a history of not investing in skills—by definition they have little education and work experience—would not respond to such incentives.
3. See Chapter 2 for a discussion of the factor analysis processes. As with the fac-

tor analysis used on skills in the entry-level job, we did not hold any *a priori* expectations about the patterns in any of the six skill groupings, but let the factor analysis determine the number of constructs in each. We used an oblique factor analysis in each area of skills.

4. The 13 skill sets in the position above entry explain between 58.2 (software) and 70.3 percent (equipment) of the variation in the observed skill requirements. Results of the factor analysis for skills used in the job above entry level are available from the author.

5. The correlation between the two canonical variables becomes the first canonical correlation, and the coefficients of the linear combinations are the canonical coefficients. Upon continued canonical correlation analysis, a second set of canonical variables is found that produces the second highest correlation coefficient. The process is continued until the number of pairs of canonical variables equals the number of variables from the smaller set. The number of canonical variables in J_2 (skill sets in positions above entry level) is smaller than that in J_1 (skill sets in entry-level positions) because the number of skill sets in the position above entry level is less than the number in the entry level. The number of variables in j_1 and j_2 (individual skills) are the same.

6

Labor Markets for Workers in Low-Skilled Positions

How Can Policies Help Workers?

I think that it starts from the vision: it's the vision shared with the employer and staff. If there are a bunch of people on different teams it's hard to see each other's vision.
—A low-wage worker

We framed this study in a conventional model of the labor market for workers in low-skilled positions. In this model, competitive forces determine employment and wages for homogeneous workers, which means workers in low-skilled positions have little job security or chance for advancement and low, undifferentiated wages. Our conventional model stands in contrast to the labor market for skilled workers, in which workers can command above-market wages for skills, climb promotional ladders, and have job security. Because markets for skilled workers do not clear with above-market wages, job queues develop for workers in skilled positions and an excess supply of workers enters the low-skilled labor market. The oversupply of homogeneous workers bids down market-based wages for workers in low-skilled positions and, as a result, workers face a flat wage profile, since firms have little incentive to provide job security or advancement.

Results of this study suggest that the conventional model of the labor market for workers in low-skilled positions does not ring true. Our study describes a market in which jobs with virtually no stated education or work experience requirements require, in actuality, a relatively broad set of skills. Firms have difficulty attracting qualified applicants for low-skilled positions and, in an attempt to locate them, use extensive recruiting and screening tools to ferret out workers with the needed skills. Processes for determining wages and promotional opportunities for workers in low-skilled positions are remarkably similar to those in the market for skilled workers: firms increase occupational wages to attract appropriately skilled workers and offer opportunities for advancement to positions above entry level requiring an increased range of skills.

These features of the labor market in which low-skilled workers toil suggest that policy prescriptions for reducing their poverty and un-employment must be grounded in skill acquisition. In this final chapter, we summarize the employers' view of the labor market for workers in low-skilled positions and provide a voice for low-skilled workers to describe the same labor market. Juxtaposing the viewpoints on the de-mand and supply sides of the labor market helps us tease out potential policy solutions to the low wages and poverty that frequently haunt workers in low-skilled positions.

THE LABOR MARKET FOR WORKERS IN LOW-SKILLED POSITIONS: THE EMPLOYER'S VIEW

Despite the idiosyncratic nuances of local areas, labor markets for workers in low-skilled positions exhibit remarkable similarities. Na-tionwide and in the BALS labor market, low-skilled jobs are concen-trated in a few industries and occupations. Three industries—1) ser-vices, 2) retail trade, and 3) manufacturing—contain three-quarters of all low-skilled jobs. Similarly, about three-quarters of all positions fall into six occupational categories: 1) administrative support, 2) produc-tion, 3) sales, 4) transportation, 5) building and grounds maintenance, and 6) food preparation and serving. The service industry alone houses about 40 percent of all low-skilled jobs by industry, and administrative support jobs make up 40 percent of all low-skilled employment by oc-cupational category.

Individuals do not need much in the way of credentials to apply for a low-skilled job. However, once hired, workers in low-skilled positions must possess a large number of skills to be successful on the job. Virtu-ally all jobs require some level of the new basic skills—English, math, problem-solving, and communication skills. Communication skills are used in virtually all low-skilled jobs, as over 90 percent require interac-tion with coworkers to accomplish a task, over 80 percent require engaging in appropriate actions at work and perceiving cues from others correctly, and about 65 percent call for dealing with customers.

Academic skills are also used heavily in low-skilled jobs. About three-quarters require an individual to read in English, to write simple sentences, and to fill out forms or logs. Over 70 percent require math (addition and subtraction). The majority of jobs require problem-solving skills: over 60 percent require the worker to identify work-related problems, prioritize tasks, or gather information. Job equipment skills are used with less frequency in low-skilled jobs than are the new basic skills. However, their *relative* use is greater in low-skilled jobs than in other jobs, as low-skilled jobs require greater levels of physical and mechanical skills than other jobs.

Thus, a puzzle exists: why are low-skilled jobs called low-skilled jobs if they require so many skills? The answer lies in a relative comparison. Low-skilled jobs require *relatively* fewer skills than other jobs. Nationwide, low-skilled jobs have significantly lower skill requirements in 64 percent of the measures of knowledges, 77 percent of the measures of skills, and 29 percent of the measures of abilities. All lower requirements of low-skilled jobs fall into areas that would be classified as new basic skills.

Both the nature and the level of skills required of the worker in a low-skilled job vary with the occupation and the industry of employment. Low-skilled jobs in office and administrative support require the highest level of skills, followed by jobs in sales. In both areas, requirements are heavily oriented toward the new basic skills. Office administration jobs require relatively high levels of English, applied math, algebra, and office equipment skills and an ability to prioritize, evaluate, lead, and communicate with customers and coworkers, while sales positions require English, applied math, and algebra skills and an ability to evaluate and communicate with customers. Low-skilled jobs in production, maintenance, and transportation require fewer of the new basic skills than office and administrative support or sales positions, but require production equipment skills and physical and mechanical skills and abilities. Production jobs require mechanical skills and small-motor, math, and problem-solving abilities, while maintenance and transportation positions require math and large-motor abilities. Food service positions require the fewest skills of any occupation for workers in low-skilled positions, although they do require large-motor abilities.

Skill requirements also differ along industry lines. The service sector houses jobs requiring the highest level of skills. Jobs in business, medical, and education establishments use English, algebra and measurement, communication with customers and coworkers, prioritizing and leadership, productivity-enhancing software, and office equipment skills. Jobs in services other than business, medical, and education require English, applied math and measurement, communication with customers and coworkers, office equipment usage, prioritizing, evaluating, and leadership. The only skills not used in this sector are computer software skills. Jobs in the business service sector use English, communication with customers and coworkers, evaluation and prioritizing, problem-solving skills, productivity enhancers and multimedia software, and office equipment. Jobs in retail trade require relatively low levels of skills, but they do require communication with customers and coworkers and applied math skills. Jobs in manufacturing use production equipment and math skills.

Perhaps because low-skilled positions use a relatively large number and variety of skills, firms face difficulties in locating qualified applicants, even when unemployment rates are high. Close to six in ten of the firms in the BALS labor market had difficulty finding qualified workers when unemployment rates exceeded 7 percent, and one in four had extreme difficulty locating qualified applicants. The stated problems in finding qualified workers suggest that firms do not view workers in low-skilled positions as homogeneous, but believe them to have enough skill heterogeneity to warrant screening applications.

Several behavioral indicators confirm that firms actively recruit and screen for specific skills in their low-skilled jobs. First, firms alter their hiring and employment processes between tight and loose labor markets in ways that are consistent with seeking specific skills in workers in low-skilled positions. As labor markets loosen, firms use less extensive recruiting methods but adopt more intensive screening methods, as would be expected if they were sifting through a greater number of applications to find workers with needed skills. Second, firms coordinate their recruiting and screening methods and adopt methods to obtain workers with skills needed in low-skilled positions.

Third, firms build promotional opportunities out of entry-level, low-skilled jobs by structuring the position above entry to require skills that expand upon the skill sets used in the entry-level job. The position above entry level uses increased levels of English and problem-solving skills in conjunction with skills used in the entry-level position, which is consistent with an expansion in duties as a lead, supervisor, or manager in the position above entry level.

Fourth, firms may be ensuring that they have a pipeline of appropriately skilled workers for the job above entry by hiring entry-level workers with skills needed in the position above it. The successful applicant for the low-skilled job has education, work experience, and English language abilities that far exceed the stated requirements for the entry-level job and closely approximate the levels needed in the job above it.

Finally, occupational wages increase in positions using skills that carry a high relative demand in the local labor market—i.e., wages rise in jobs using skill sets that firms have difficulty obtaining. Institutional factors, particularly unionization, also increase occupational wages for workers in low-skilled positions; the influence of institutional factors is nearly as strong as that of skills.

THE LABOR MARKET FOR WORKERS IN LOW-SKILLED JOBS: THE WORKER'S VIEW

The view of the labor market presented by BALS employers contrasts sharply with the one presented by workers—both potential and incumbent—in low-skilled jobs. Workers typically view the labor market as one with an excess supply of job seekers, even when labor markets are tight, and see employers as having their pick of the job-seeking throng. The low-skilled workplace appears extremely inhospitable to workers attempting to juggle work, family, economic security, and daily survival in a global market that leaves them increasingly isolated from the middle-class culture to which they aspire (Munger 2002). The balancing act is made more difficult for the segment of the population struggling with mental illness, substance abuse, domestic violence, and homelessness (Rangarajan 2001). In such a world, the incentive offered by low wages to enter the labor market can lose out to the tug of relationships and the obstacles posed by an abusive home environment, mean streets, and seemingly capricious work rules and government support (DeParle 2004). Still, many of the working poor exhibit a strong work ethic despite their limited ability to obtain employment and to move beyond their dead-end job (Newman 1999). Such individuals may need a job but not be able to engage in long-term training, even if it is publicly funded, because of the tugs on their daily lives. Like most of us, some workers in low-skilled jobs have made bad choices. When a middle-class worker makes an unwise choice, there are safety nets in place. For a low-skilled worker, an unwise path taken in the face of bad fortune frequently leaves the worker with little control over the outcome (Shipler 2004).

Low-income residents in the community used for the BALS Household Survey tell of the tension between work and life struggles faced by workers in low-skilled positions. They eloquently expressed these views in five focus groups, which were structured by BALS researchers to elicit qualitative information from individuals working in or applying for low-skilled jobs about their work, education, and support systems.[1] Focus group participants were recruited from case files of local nonprofit, community-based social service agencies. Each group was made up of individuals who were similar in age to one another; only two of the groups contained adults (aged 23 to 45). One of the adult groups (with eight members) was interviewed in Spanish. Information from the 14 adult focus group participants paints a powerful picture of low-skilled workers' perceptions about the labor market and the skills needed to be successful workforce participants. We present here the voices of workers in low-skilled jobs as they talk about their experiences and frustrations in their work life.[2]

On What You Do

Focus group participants were asked to describe their experiences working (for pay or as a volunteer), what they thought made them successful, and what made it difficult for them to be successful. Participants, in discussing their low-skilled positions, describe a work life that is intertwined with family, kids, and community. In their voices, here is what they said:

> Back in my country I was a businesswoman. I had a small business of repairing of electrical components and also electrical appliances. I used to run the business, and when I moved here I didn't have the permit to work. I raised my children and my family. I have four

children. I married young, and that was quite a career in itself raising those four children. And when my children were growing up we stayed at home—that was still in that era—and [duties included] cooking and sewing. I had to make all of my children's clothes, and was always baking. And then running back and forth to my mother, helping my mother when she [was] sick, helping, always giving a hand. Then I finally went to work. My first job was as a certified nurse's aide at a hospital in North [San Diego] County. That was five years there—I think five years there; it was quite an interesting experience. Then I went back east and I was there for a couple of years working as [an] industrial machine operator, which is a fantastic, interesting job. I was doing piecework, but to operate those machines you have to be quick; it goes with the blink of an eye. There's a technique that one has to learn . . . for piecework, and you only get paid for what you produce. So it was fascinating and I learned it, and became very good at it, and I rose up within the factory there. Of course my children would say, "Mommy, why are you doing this?" It was a challenge and I met that challenge; I was very proud of myself. It was a wonderful experience; interesting people I worked with. Then I came back to California, and then I took training at the computer center in Alameda. Then I signed up with [a social program], which is for older folks like me trying to get in[to] the workforce. Through them I came to a local community agency as a receptionist. Then, when a position opened up for an advocate, I pursued that opportunity. That's why I'm an advocate now, which I enjoy very much. The longer I stay at this job, the more I learn, and I feel more comfortable and feel I'm gaining experience and being what people's families' resources are for—to meet people's needs. It's gratifying. I enjoy it.

I kind of volunteer for [a] nonprofit agency in the community. I do it for the kids—at the present time I'm working at their school. I'm hoping that in time the neighborhood will learn how to respect their own property and their surroundings; at present they're not very good at it. So I guess what my main interest in it is, [is] the children. There [are] a lot of children [doing things] real gang-related, and I would like to see them be successful in life and not end up in juvenile hall.

Are we talking about all the jobs that we have had? Well, I lived here my whole life; it started with probably a paper route, all the way to working with the school district. As far as volunteering goes, I started volunteer[ing] with the focused curriculum in the high school, and that was pretty fulfilling actually, and basically the program helps kids prepare for college—underserved and underprivileged [children]. And I have had the unique opportunity to work with a young kid since about tenth grade, and he just started his first year here at the local university. So it's been a pretty good experience.

I'm a housewife. I have never worked. I also volunteer time in the school.

I work at a retail clothing store and volunteer at a nonprofit agency located at a neighborhood elementary school.

Eight years working [at] an overnight mail delivery company, bakery, electronics [store], and I used to do volunteer work in San Rafael.

I worked as [a] janitor in a hotel, volunteer at [a] school cafeteria, and also at a Parent Institute.

I['ve] been in the same job for five years [furniture store].

Four years in [a] retail store and 12 years in a furniture store.

Pizza parlor, a corporate motor school, and volunteer for a Parent Institute.

I was a Telex operator. [Now] I work an order desk at a wallpaper company. When I first got out of school I went into [the] armed services. I was a crypto tech, which is the intelligence.

On What Helps You in the Workplace

Workers in low-skilled jobs described how a strong work ethic, discipline, a good attitude, teamwork, punctuality, and enjoying what one does helped make them successful in the workplace. They gave a general sense that they believe that workers get more out of the workplace if they put more into it. Relatively few mentioned the need for skills for success in the workplace.

I think your attitude and how much you want to be there [helps you in the workplace]. Sometimes you have to be there, but if you make it so that you want to be there, it makes it to go a lot quicker. As far as the day, I think that you pull more out of it when you enjoy being there.

So you should have a good smile [which helps you in the workplace]. I know what [it] is like to hear gossip all day at work. It's nothing nice. On the way to work you think, "I['ve] got to hear so-and-so talk all day long about whoever." I do my work. I interact with people. If other people have fun too it makes it a lot better.

I have worked in a variety of settings. When I worked in retail I found that when you are on part of a team it can be really basic, like a reward system. Like [when] I was on the safety team we built a camaraderie. It made it more fun: at the end of the month the team with the most safety got a $25 certificate. When you have two teams working on a common goal [it spurs competition], even though it was just [for] a grocery store [certificate]. After that we joined [a] softball league, which builds more of a camaraderie. When you don't have those things worked into an organization you get back to "I'm just going to do my job." [But] when you share a vision [and] a common goal like with working with non-profits, [it helps]. It is very important to establish your goal so you don't feel like you're by yourself. Then you feel resentment—you feel like you're overworked and underpaid, [as if you're] doing the stuff from the heart. And you don't have that built in[to the compensation].

I feel it's not like being really screwed over. At times people do get screwed over. There is other stuff, if you really knew. In the cases that I have been around, people got screwed over.

—I agree with you, but I feel that it comes from yourself not investigating what's going on.

Agility [of mind]: to pay attention to every detail.

My desire to surpass [expectations]—be always on time, go to work every day.

My economic needs.

The desire to work.

Work the same way with or without supervision.

Produce the work that is necessary.

Work hard and always do your best.

Know how to drive and [have] a clean driving record. Be punctual and follow orders.

Discipline.

On What Makes It Difficult for You in the Workplace

Focus group participants acknowledged that an attitude and a work ethic lead to success in the workplace. However, they struggle with problems in their work life, and they seem to place the cause of their problems outside their control. Work permits and discrimination are societal-level issues that focus group participants feel create difficulties in their work life. At a more mundane level, problems with coworkers, employers demanding too much, a lack of training, miscommunications, and a belief that some people don't want them to succeed make the day-to-day work difficult. Only one focus group participant placed the blame for workplace difficulties on what might be construed as a lack of skills: not being able to speak English.

> [It's hard for me to work because] the employer demands too much from me. Four months ago I [did] not produce the same as in the beginning. But it's because the employer asks me to work more and more. Why am I going to produce more when another employee works less and get[s] [paid] more?

> [It's hard for me to work because of] people who do not let you succeed because of jealousy. You always find people that make you look bad. But I had always been a talkative person, and that's the reason why I got fired. But I always say, "I do not work with my mouth."

> The coworkers tease and threaten you without a reason. In one occasion a female worker tried to stab me with a pair of scissors. I asked for an explanation from my boss but he just replied, "Don't pay attention to that woman, she's crazy." The employers don't do anything to solve the problems.

> I do cleaning at a community agency and those ladies are just rude, so that makes things difficult.

They don't have patience to train new people.

People not wanting to help you succeed.

Racial discrimination.

Being discriminated [against] by your own race.

Miscommunication, lack of understanding.

I have found that not having a permit to work in this country it is hard to get a job.

Your immigration status.

Not being able to speak English.

On the Knowledge and Skills Needed

Focus group participants were asked about the knowledge and skills they felt were needed to get a job, keep a job, and get promoted. Getting the job seemed to be of utmost importance in their minds, as a fair amount of discussion centered on interviewing skills and external factors (e.g., references, immigration papers) they believed would help them get the job. The skills emphasized were determination in the job search, personality, and presentation of self. Self-esteem, sense of character, and willingness to learn were discussed in general terms as being important. Many participants voiced concern about (presumably) low-skilled individuals not having a strong sense of character or self, and some painted a somewhat combative picture of the workplace.

> When I was little [the home] helped me build up my esteem and the sense of character. I think that it's monumental as far as knowledge and skills . . . What I think that you need to go up the ladder is, one, attitude, and, two, personality. When I work with students I [tell] them that [their] personality will get them a long way. Skills and knowledge will come but who you are is what got you in the door. All the things will come to you if you are willing to learn them. So if you have a good presentation of yourself, your self-esteem comes [into] play, then your character ties in. Then everything else comes out.

I think that it is how much you put into it. You have to draw the line: you don't want to go above and beyond the call of duties. If you put too much in you might get taken advantage of. Then you walk out feeling bad, so you get rebellious and you do not get your job done right. And you just won't feel appreciated.

I would like to make the comment that when a child first starts to walk [he has an] interest in it. Just like work—if there is no interest in it you won't put your full effort into it. And for surviving you will have to take those jobs. People who are around me I should find interesting; then I can [apply that] to my job.

Have connections with somebody that is already working at that place.

Have somebody to give good references about you.

Have a legal status [immigration papers].

Be determined to get that job.

Fight to achieve your goal.

I think it's the willingness to learn. If you're not willing to learn, then you're not going to go anywhere.

On How Life Affects Getting and Keeping a Job

Participants were asked about all the things in their home life that affect the ability to be successful in their work life. Their answers provided insights into their day-to-day struggles with child care, transportation, and a street culture of drugs, violence, and alcohol—all of which may funnel energy away from the workplace.

If your spouse drinks too much alcohol.

When your spouse doesn't help you with the children's care and homework. Your husband thinks that his responsibility is to go to the work and bring the money home.

When a family member has gang-related problems.

Being a single mother, and not having enough time for your work and children.

Child care, and trust[ing] the person in charge of your children.

Drugs, gangs, violence. Worrying for your kids' safety.

Transportation—when you don't have a car—and your kids' transportation from home to school.

When you can't afford child care.

When I am at work I do not think about the problems at home.

My son, who is 18 year[s] old, is working for the first time . . . [so] I do not have any problems.

On Going to School

Since most of the focus group participants did not have much education, they were asked about their schooling, what factors made schooling hard for them, and what factors made it easy for them. Many talked about the negative feedback they received about school from people in authority positions in the school or in their home. Some participants spoke of experiencing fear and rejection with respect to schooling. A few participants broke down in tears during the discussion. Few mentioned gaining knowledge and skills in school. When asked what they would tell teens about school, they all offered advice about staying in school and studying but provided no specifics about strategies for doing so (e.g., go to college, get knowledge and skills).

When I first went to school I was really afraid because I did not want to go to school, because I was beaten because I did not know how to write ABCs. My mother was not educated so I wanted to be educated. So, when I went to the school, for the first three or four years I was very afraid. I knew the things to say but I was so afraid of speaking out. So in my class I sat with all the fear. And now I realize that, for a child, they need support.

I feel scared and I just started going to class again. I start to get all upset—I guess [from] the anxiety of the adventure. I was brought up in a business so when I was not in school I was working. Summers were the same way; I worked all summer. So I did not mind school, was a pretty good student. I had five brothers; we all went through school and graduated. [The parents] really did not push the college part. Don't know if they did not want to pay for it by putting all the money [toward it that] we earned them for their own retirement. That was one of the reasons I went [in]to the military. I do not think that it was fear; the only time I got smacked was when I did something wrong. I was so afraid to speak, but I knew [the answer] from the inside. I just was . . . scared to speak.

I was never really into school, but I liked school. I liked learning. I loved my history classes because we got to color in the continents. In high school we did a motivation thing in school. It was a big deal I guess because I wanted more out of myself. I once had a teacher that told me that I would never amount to anything in life, and I just want to prove that person wrong.

—I had a counselor tell me that.

—I had a principal tell me that.

—People like that are the ones who encourage me to want more in life, to go on and prove them wrong. People who have set judgments on me. I knew a lot of my friends from back in junior high. We would talk about what we wanted to do in life, and some of them would be like, "Oh, after high school I want to be married." I was the one who did not want to be married—I wanted to break all the preconceptions that people had about me because I was a female and the culture I came from. A lot of girls in Mexico get married at 16, you have kids, and your husband is twice your age. You're a mother and a wife for the rest of your life. That is something that I did not want to become.

It saddened me to see people who couldn't read.

On Advice to Teens about School

Reach the goals that were impossible for us.

Study hard and stay away from gangs.

Don't get married or get pregnant at a young age.

Keep studying for a better future.

Unlike us, get a good education.

Be professionals.

Although residents in the BALS neighborhood voice frustration about the labor market they face, their dissatisfaction is focused on external forces. In contrast to employers, who focus on skill needs in workers, low-income individuals rarely mention skills—or lack there-of—as underlying their workforce problems or as roadblocks to their moving up a career ladder. Instead they frequently link workforce issues to personal or family problems: gangs, violence, family relationships, and a lack of self-esteem. Some focus group members point to issues in the broader society as creating obstacles for them: immigrant status, discrimination, and the lack of a work permit. Still others point to seemingly overpowering internal problems in the workplace that prevent success: gossip, workers getting an unfair shake or getting taken advantage of, or impatient employers that fail to provide training.

Successes also seem to be externally defined. Even though some focus group participants talk about the need for attention to details, determination, willingness to learn, and the ability to operate a machine as skills that make one successful in the workplace, most of the discussion about what it takes to get ahead is not centered on learned skills, nor did focus group participants mention the need to get workplace skills while in school. Instead, focus group participants discuss teamwork and camaraderie as important to workplace success, implying that these factors organically arise in the workplace and are not in the worker's control. The need for self-esteem—a good attitude, personality, and presentation of self—is frequently brought up as an essential characteristic for the workplace, yet as a characteristic that is suppressed in the home or in the schools.

While some members of the focus group clearly believe that individuals are responsible for their work life, many others seem to believe that forces beyond their control create their difficulties. This is not meant to diminish the problems encountered by workers in low-skilled positions. Rather, it is meant to illustrate the overwhelming nature of the battles facing them. Low wages leave them without transportation or money for child care and make it difficult to become a reliable worker. Worries about children joining gangs or facing violence in their schools or about alcoholic spouses distract them from their determination to make good at work. From this vantage point, the obstacles to getting ahead are indeed outside of their control. For even if they were able to gain additional skills, they would still face the challenges imposed by a low-income life without safety nets. Their advice to their children implies that they believe youth have the ability to control their future. "Stay in school, don't do what we did, avoid gangs and early pregnancies" is advice that could easily be interpreted as pleas for youth to take control before it is too late.

THE SECOND-CHANCE POLICY SOLUTION: WIA TRAINING

Employers voice frustration at their difficulty in finding qualified applicants for low-skilled positions, most probably because they see a disjuncture between the skills they need and those that job applicants and workers supply. Firms use economic incentives—increased wages and promotional opportunities—to entice workers in low-skilled positions to invest in the skills needed to perform satisfactorily on the job. Individuals voice frustration about the social forces that inhibit their ability to become successful workers and earn sufficient wages. Their daily struggle with family, cultural differences at a middle-class workplace, and economic survival make it difficult if not impossible for many to see how their skill set may not mesh with the skill sets needed by employers, how gaining skills might lead to opportunities beyond what is currently available, and how acquiring skills might be possible given their current life circumstances.

The disjuncture between the employers' and the workers' view of the low-skilled labor market could be bridged by working with individuals to build skills that are in demand in the local labor market, a logical conclusion from our study and one that was put forth in the School-to-Work Opportunity Act (STWOA), the Temporary Assistance for Needy Families (TANF) funding, and the Workforce Investment Act (WIA). The STWOA attempted to link skill development in high school students to local labor market needs. It met with modest success. TANF attempted to provide short-term training to quickly move welfare recipients into the local labor market. It succeeded in getting welfare recipients into work, but these individuals generally do not have self-sufficient wages, job stability, or positive long-term impacts (Greenberg et al. 2004). WIA training programs generally have positive returns for adult women but less consistent returns for adult men and youth (Friedlander, Greenberg, and Robins 1997; Greenberg, Michalopoulos, and Robins 2003; Grubb 1996; LaLonde 1995), and research suggests that per-trainee investments and earnings gains are small (Bloom et al. 1994).[3]

These modest payoffs for building skills that are (presumably) in demand in the local labor market seem to be at odds with the findings of this study. One possibility for the discrepancy is that, in reality, programs do not provide skills training in areas of demand, a proposition examined by Rodecker (2004) for the nation as a whole. As he notes, "A rigorous definition of what constitutes an in-demand occupation is not forthcoming in the [WIA] legislation; rather, states and local Workforce Investment Boards are charged with the responsibility of identifying in-demand occupations based on labor market occupations."

Rodecker compares total job openings in the nation to WIA-provided training across the nation and demonstrates inconsistencies. For the nation as a whole, he finds that WIA adult training programs overtrain (i.e., provide too much training) for computer operators and truck drivers and undertrain (provide too little training) for retail salespersons, stock clerks, and order fillers.

The BALS data afford a unique opportunity to determine the consistency between WIA training and employers' stated needs in a local labor market, so as to be able to tell whether programs provide training for in-demand occupations, as stated in the legislation (section 134. d.4.G.iii): "Training services provided . . . shall be directly linked to occupations that are in-demand in the local area" (WIA 1998). We use standardized data from the WIA records to determine the occupational training provided with WIA funds to individuals in the BALS counties and its consistency with low-skilled job openings as defined by the BALS employers.[4] This comparison is a luxury afforded by the uniqueness of the BALS data, for it is only because of the information from the BALS Phone Survey that we have a listing of data for entry-level, low-skilled jobs in the three-county labor market.

Individuals in our local labor market that use WIA funds for training fit the general profile of those eligible for BALS-type jobs (Table 6.1). Only about 31 percent have more than a high school education, and only about 66 percent have English proficiency. While Bay Area WIA-funded training appears to be targeted at those who need it, the services

Table 6.1 Low-Skilled Jobs and WIA Training in the Bay Area Local Labor Market

	% BALS jobs	WIA training
Demographics		
Average age	—	41.8
Percent male	—	42.4
Percent limited English	—	33.6
Race/Ethnicity		
Percent Hispanic	—	18.5
Percent Asian	—	39.0
Percent black	—	17.4
Percent American Indian/Alaskan/Hawaiian	—	1.7
Percent white (not Hispanic)	—	23.3
Multiple (not including Hispanic)	—	0.3
Location (county)		
Percent Alameda	61.4	27.7**
Percent San Francisco	23.9	53.1**
Percent San Joaquin	14.8	19.3**
Highest grade completed		
Percent 12 or less	—	67.8
Percent with GED	—	1.1
Percent 13–15	—	17.0
Percent 16 or more	—	14.0
Occupation (of job or WIA training)		
Areas of highest occupational employment		
Office and administrative support	41.3	23.4**
Production	11.1	4.0**
Food preparation and serving	9.8	3.8**
Sales and related	8.5	0.8**
Building and grounds cleaning/maintenance	7.6	13.2**
Transportation and material moving	7.1	14.9**
Other occupations		
Personal care and service	2.8	0.8**
Installation, maintenance, and repair	2.1	1.5
Education, training, and library	1.9	0.7**
Protective service	1.7	0.1**
Construction and extraction	1.2	5.1**

Table 6.1 (continued)

	% BALS jobs	WIA training
Health care support	1.1	12.7**
Health care practitioner/technical	0.6	1.5**
Business and financial	0.5	0.8
Farming, fishing, and forestry	0.5	0.0**
Computer and mathematical	0.4	10.4**
Community and social services	0.4	0.4
Art, design, entertainment, sports, and media	0.4	2.4**
Management	0.3	2.0**
Architecture and engineering	0.1	1.7**
Military	0.1	0.0
Life, physical, and social science	0.0	0.1
Legal	0.0	0.1
N	2,052	2,099

NOTE: WIA data are from the 2002 Workforce Investment Act Standardized Record Data (WIASRD) and contain information only on individuals in Alameda, San Francisco, and San Joaquin counties that received occupational training. N varies slightly with item-specific missing data. ** indicates significant ($p \leq 0.05$) differences between the samples. — = not available.
SOURCE: BALS Phone Survey (HIRE 2006); 2002 WIASRD (USDOL 2004).

that participants receive may not mirror those needed in low-skilled positions in the local labor market. In fact, a disjuncture exists between the occupations of entry-level, low-skilled jobs in the local area and the occupations in which WIA provides training: only 60 percent of WIA participants receive training in one of the seven occupations containing 85 percent of the entry-level, low-skilled jobs in the BALS local labor market.

Our comparison suggests that WIA provides less training than needed in office and administrative support occupations, production jobs, and food and sales positions. Undertraining for food and sales positions may be justified, given their relatively low wages. However, both office jobs and administrative support and production jobs pay higher-than-average wages in the BALS labor market, and, as a result, the undertraining in these areas may hinder an individual's efforts to gain low-skilled employment at relatively high wages.

WIA programs in the BALS labor market may provide more training than needed for building and transportation, health-care support, and computer and mathematical occupations. Because computer and math skills are needed frequently in the position above entry level, overtraining in these areas may enhance the program participants' chances for a promotion, assuming the skills do not decay (Lillard and Tan 1992). However, building and grounds cleaning and maintenance, transportation, and health-care support are areas in which WIA's overtraining holds less potential for use, since skills are not in short supply in the local labor market.

So why might providers train in areas of oversupply? Programs receive funding based, in part, on employment rates of participants. Employment rates lie significantly above average in building and grounds cleaning and maintenance and in health-care support occupations—areas of overtraining—and somewhat below average in office and administrative support, the typical occupation with jobs available in the BALS labor market and an area of undertraining (Table 6.2).[5] Thus, even though over 40 percent of the low-skilled, entry-level jobs in the BALS labor market are in office and administrative support and even though these jobs pay above-average wages, publicly funded training may not be targeted at this area because employment rates after training are relatively low. One explanation for this phenomenon has to do with the relatively high skills required in office and administrative support. It may be that the skill deficits of trainees are too high to allow them to acquire the necessary knowledge and skills within the allotted time frame of most publicly funded training programs. Analysis presented in Chapter 3 suggests that office and administrative support jobs require relatively high levels of English, applied math, algebra, and office equipment skills and an ability to prioritize, evaluate, lead, and communicate with customers and coworkers.

Providing such skills may be difficult within WIA's relatively short training period. Because individuals with limited English (who make up one-third of the WIA-trained individuals in the BALS labor market), few math skills, or low levels of critical thinking and interpersonal skills may have difficulty gaining the skills needed for office administration positions within a six-month training period, providers do not train in these areas. Building and grounds cleaning and maintenance, and perhaps health-care support occupations, require far fewer skills.

Table 6.2 Employment Probabilities and Types of WIA-Funded Training in the Bay Area Local Labor Market

Occupational training	Percent employed			Sample size (after training)		
	First quarter	Third quarter	Fifth quarter	First quarter	Third quarter	Fifth quarter
Computer and mathematical science	74.4	65.5	57.4	133	116	68
Health care support	86.3**	83.6**	75.8**	168	140	91
Food preparation and serving–related	81.1	73.5	72.8	53	49	22
Building and grounds cleaning and maintenance	90.5**	81.8**	72.6**	179	159	95
Office and administrative support	70.4	65.4	70.0	307	254	130
Construction and extraction	66.7	55.7	37.9**	66	61	29
Production	74.5	61.9	50.0**	55	42	22
Transportation and material moving	76.9	65.8	44.0**	186	149	50
Total	73.8	68.4	60.1	1,609	1,385	798

NOTE: Data are from the 2002 WIASRD and contain information only on individuals in Alameda, San Francisco, and San Joaquin counties that received occupational training. Results reflect occupations with 50 or more individuals reporting employment status in the first quarter after training. ** indicates significant ($p \leq 0.05$) differences between the probability of employment for individuals in a specific occupational training and the aggregate probability of employment for all individuals as measured by a t-test.
SOURCE: USDOL (2004).

Program providers may be able to bridge the skill gap between program participants and employers' needs more quickly for jobs in these areas, and, as a result, employment rates for participants will be higher than in office and administrative support.

POLICY IMPLICATIONS

What do these results suggest for policy? Our study has repeatedly illustrated the need for skills in low-skilled jobs; its results show that employers perceive a gap between the skills needed on the job and those held by individuals applying for the job. Public schools—an individual's first chance for obtaining needed skills—do not provide all individuals with needed skills. Publicly funded training programs—an individual's second chance for obtaining skills—may not be of sufficient length to bridge the skill gap between program participants and job requirements. Furthermore, adults in low-skilled positions face life circumstances that may make it difficult for them to invest the time needed to bridge the skill gap. If they fail again and again, second chance programs become costly for both individuals and society.

These results have several implications for public policy. First and foremost, basic skills must be built in our public schools. Over three-quarters of the jobs available to youth after they leave high school require some type of reading or writing (of English), and over 70 percent require addition and subtraction. Unfortunately, differences in quality exist in our public schools, and because of that not all individuals take away basic academic and social skills from school (Card and Krueger 1992b). Until all students have access to basic social and academic skill provision in public schools, the problems that plague employers and workers in low-skilled jobs will continue. Obtaining basic skills in school also reduces the complications that arise from obtaining them later in life when adult responsibilities increase the cost of their acquisition. Because basic social and academic skills are needed by employers at much higher levels than more specific job skills, public policy must focus on providing high quality schooling, good work habits, and basic social skills to all students. If individuals acquire basic academic and social skills in schools, the labor market can build job-specific skills.

An intended side effect of such an emphasis would be the increased probability of college attendance, since individuals increasingly are turning to postsecondary education to gain the requisite academic skills and work habits necessary to succeed.

Academic skills are used in virtually all entry-level positions and increase the probability of employment for youth (Maxwell, forthcoming); hence, they must be a critical component of any educational or training program that sets as one of its goals youth employability. However, our study shows that jobs available to youth as they leave high school require the new basic skills of communication and problem-solving at relatively high levels. Over 80 percent require workers to work with others, act appropriately at work, and be perceptive of others, and over 60 percent require dealing with customers, problem-solving collaboratively, identification of work-related problems, prioritizing tasks, and gathering information.

Building new basic skills, including academics, in high school may be a necessary but not a sufficient condition for moving youth from school to work, since the skills needed by firms may not exactly fit with those targeted for learning in schools. If curricula emphasize academic learning, high schools will want to ensure that skills learned in school can be transferred easily to the workplace. In the BALS labor market, building simple English skills, which have a high relative demand, means making sure students can read written instructions, manuals, computer printouts, contracts, and agreements; write simple sentences, short notes, and simple memos; and fill out forms and record data or time into a log or chart. Students' communication skills would include choosing appropriate words and manner of expression at work, perceiving verbal and nonverbal cues from others, interacting with coworkers to accomplish a task, and dealing with customers. Prioritization skills would include prioritizing tasks and identifying work-related problems. Because many of these skills are specific to a workplace environment and, as a result, may not be the target of direct instruction in school, schools may want to ensure that the general reading, writing, and problem-solving skills taught in school can be transferred into the workplace.

Workforce readiness skills are also universally required in the low-skilled jobs (e.g., acceptable behavior at work), but they may be ubiquitous among entry-level workers. Schools should therefore focus on building these skills only if they do not exist in the schools' student population. Without workforce readiness skills, youth will not be competitive with other workers in low-skilled jobs; however, the provision of such skills may be superfluous in some student populations. Finally, most specific workplace skills are needed in relatively few entry-level, low-skilled jobs and are held by a relatively large percentage of the population (at least in the BALS labor market). Building these skills in schools may be for naught since relatively few employers put them to use. In fact, because individuals may be able to obtain workplace skills while on the job, their acquisition during school, especially if it comes in place of academic skills, may disadvantage students once they become labor-force participants. A better use of program resources would be for building on skills used more universally—academic and social skills.

Focusing schools on building academic and workplace skills for education and labor market success was a cornerstone of the STWOA. Unfortunately, its emphasis on workplace skills may have been flawed. School-to-work programs integrated workplace skills into academic instruction in an attempt to build both sets of skills. Results of this study suggest that this integration benefits future workers only if it increases academic skills and may harm individuals if it builds workplace skills at the expense of academic skills. Phrased somewhat differently, the premise of school-to-work programs is valid only if workplace and academic skills are production complements. It is fatally flawed if they are production substitutes. In this respect the foundation set forth in *A Nation at Risk*, which the National Commission on Excellence in Education came out with in 1983, was more on target, but that report failed to capture the importance of our schools in building communication and the workforce readiness skills needed by employers.

The No Child Left Behind Act of 2001 (NCLB) focuses on accountability, freedom of choice, and scientifically based instruction, all of which place indirect emphasis on skill acquisition. The emphasis on testing and accountability may divert resources away from skill acquisition, however, if resources are moved toward achieving mandates required by legislation and away from academics. Under the worst-case scenario, schools will start playing numbers games to hide poor performance, inflating grades so that parents falsely believe their children are learning, and replacing longer-term, lower-visibility skill building with quick-fix, high visibility results (e.g., capital improvements, safety).

Even with improved public schools, some students will not gain basic academic and social skills while in school, making publicly funded (second chance) job training programs essential. Because large gaps may exist between the academic and workforce readiness skills held by low-skilled adults and those needed by employers, job training programs must be available if skill gaps are to be closed. Unfortunately, our understanding about what workers in job training programs need is in its infancy (D'Amico 2005).

Results of this study suggest that job training programs might want to shift their emphasis in three ways. First, the current policy strategy of back-to-work should be restructured into one of skill-building. While work itself can alter individuals' self-esteem (Gottschalk 2005), the failure of such programs to have lasting impacts is troublesome. Results of this study suggest a greater long-term impact would result from building skills that are in demand in the local labor market.

Second, short-term training needs to be expanded. Most second-chance training programs are of short duration and receive modest funding. Programs must be cognizant of the fact that individuals may have spent years letting basic skills atrophy or may never have built basic skills needed in the local labor market in which they locate as adults (skills such as English or workplace behavior that matches U.S. expectations). Under such circumstances, individuals cannot expect to gain needed skills in only six months. For these individuals, basic skills—English, math, communication, and problem-solving—must be developed and fostered over a longer period of time. WIA represents a step in consolidating services under one roof and in providing a local labor market focus, but it does not provide the necessary time that some need for basic skill acquisition. LaLonde (1995, p. 149) summarizes the success of job training programs succinctly: "The best summary of the evidence about the impact of past [job training] programs is that we got what we paid for." Training for individuals without basic skills must be long enough to ensure that program participants' skill levels reach the level needed by employers. For individuals without rudimentary academic, English, or workplace communication skills, long-term interventions may be necessary.

Third, holistic programs must be developed to reduce dropout rates. Heckman, Hohmann, and Smith (2000) illustrate the dramatic rate of program dropout. The focus group participants in this research hint at the difficulties faced by low-skilled individuals in meeting work or training obligations. Taken together, these results suggest that a holistic approach to skill-building is needed. Second-chance programs must be grounded in a broader system of support. Adults not gaining necessary skills while in school often find themselves faced with a need for training that conflicts with their need to provide care for their children, their ability to find reliable transportation, their lack of funds for training investments, and their worries about safety. For individuals in low-skilled positions to engage effectively in training, they must overcome these challenges. Individuals with relatively few skills, unlike their middle-class counterparts, may not have the economic ability to afford good-quality child care, reliable transportation, training, and housing in safe neighborhoods. They require economic support to meet these needs while investing in skills.

Once individuals acquire the basic skills needed for low-skilled employment, support must continue, since the entry-level wages will not be sufficient to overcome child care, transportation, and safety concerns outside work. Policies must provide monetary support to workers in low-skilled positions until entry-level, low-skilled workers gain a solid foothold in the workplace. Providing economic and social support must enhance the incentives for skill-building, not replace them. The holistic approach of second-chance skill acquisition must tie economic rewards to either training or employment, not use such rewards to replace them, since safety nets or income support can reduce incentives for individuals to engage in skill-building or employment. Potential policies might include such things as wage supplements or subsidies to employers or tax credits for low-wage workers, since individuals would only receive such benefits if working, thereby creating an incentive to work.

Focus group participants also suggested that gaining employment creates another host of difficulties, this one embodied in a seemingly capricious work environment. Workplace regulations, grievance procedures, and antidiscrimination regulations can help alleviate employer-created unfair treatment or hostile work environments. However, capriciousness often lies in the eye of the beholder, and comments by focus group participants suggest that some complaints may merely be disgruntled workers griping (e.g., their references to being asked to work too hard). In such cases, both schooling and training programs must instill an appropriate work ethic and a sense of appropriate workplace behavior in participants—in other words, basic workforce readiness.

As well, appropriately skilled individuals searching for low-skilled positions must be able to find employment, a possibility that is greater with tight labor markets. Chapter 4 showed that employers loosen hiring restrictions in tight labor markets, which benefits workers in low-skilled positions. Even a rising tide may not be able to lift the boats of individuals without basic skills, but it can increase employment and advancement potential for individuals that have invested in appropriate labor market skills. Economic policies that create tight labor markets will help such workers.

Finally, low-skilled workers must realize that lifelong learning is real. If individuals in low-skilled positions want to advance beyond entry level, they must continue to develop new skills. Promotional opportunities are widely available for individuals in low-skilled jobs, but the jobs above entry level require increased skills, particularly in English and problem-solving. Workers must be open to continuous learning and skill-investing throughout their work life, and training for skill improvement must be made available from both employers and public sources. The foundation for building skills is best laid in our schools, in part because the time spent building foundation skills for lifelong learning is a luxury available mainly to youth. The strongest job advancement program we can develop, therefore, is building programs in schools that develop strong basic academic and social skills and foster a desire to continuously expand skills for workplace success. The second strongest is allowing individuals a second chance at gaining such skills. It's a long-term strategy, and one that we cannot afford to ignore.

Notes

1. Of the three focus groups that did not contain adults, two contained middle-school youth and one contained high school–aged youth. Although the focus groups were held on September 15, 2001, four days after the World Trade Center disaster, facilitators and their assistants all agreed that the participants' discussion in the focus group was affected little by these events. All focus groups were audiotaped and the sessions were transcribed in the language in which the focus group was held. Spanish sessions were translated into English for purposes of reporting.

2. Not all comments are presented. We selected for inclusion the most typical comments and eliminated redundancy in presentation.
3. Per-capita investments generally ranged between $1,000 and $1,300, with annual earnings increases of $850 (in 1993 dollars). As of this writing, the WIA impact study has not been funded.
4. We use the 2002 Workforce Investment Act Title 1-B Standardized Record Data (WIASRD) for individuals undertaking training from one of the four Workforce Investment Boards (WIBs) in the BALS counties (USDOL 2004). For comparison to BALS data, we use the occupation for which individuals received training and their employment status (i.e., whether or not they were employed) in the first, third, and fifth quarter after training was completed. WIBs are required to report such information to receive WIA funding.
5. Table 6.2 shows that 26.2 percent of participants in our local labor market were not employed in the first quarter after training and 39.9 percent were not employed in the fifth quarter after training.

Appendix A

Background Tables and Variable Construction

Table A.1 Mapping Skills

A.1.a Reading and Writing English

Skill	Employer skill set	Employer Survey questions	Household Survey question
Read written instructions, safety warnings, product labels, shipping labels, invoices/work orders, logs, and journals	Simple English	1, 3, 4, 5, 11, 13, 14	7A
Read forms, memos, and letters	Simple English	9, 12	7B
Read maps	Not used	2	7D
Read manuals, computer printout, contracts, and agreements	Simple English	6, 8, 10	7C
Read telephone book	Not used	7	7E
Print or write simple sentences, or write short notes and simple memos	Simple English	1,3	8A
Take telephone messages accurately	Not used	2	8F
Write letters using correct structure and sentence style	Complex English	4	8B
Proofread	Complex English	5	8E
Fill out forms, record data or time into log or chart	Simple English	6, 8	8D
Organize information into a brief written report	Complex English	7	8C

NOTE: The question from the Household Survey asks, "How well can you . . . (in English)?" with the options being "very well," "somewhat well," "not well," and "don't know." Surveyors inserted the phrases from the leftmost column of this table into the question when asking respondents. Variables are binary, with a 1 indicating "very well" and a 0 indicating all other choices.

SOURCE: BALS Employer Survey and BALS Household Survey (HIRE 2006).

A.1.b Math

Skill	Employer skill set	Household Survey question
Perform addition and subtraction computations	Not used	9A
Perform multiplication and division computations	Applied math	9B
Use ratios, fractions, decimals, or percentages	Algebra	9C
Estimate or round off numbers	Algebra	9D
Solve simple equations	Algebra	9E
Make change	Applied math	9F
Compute or figure discounts, markups, or selling price	Applied math	9G
Interpret data from graphs, tables, or charts	Algebra	9H
Perform simple measurements (e.g., length, volume)	Measurement	9I
Use measurement instruments (e.g., ruler, scale)	Measurement	9J
Use equipment such as a calculator, cash register, or business machine	Applied math	9K

NOTE: Question 45 of the Employer Survey asks, "How well can you . . . (without any calculator or computer)?" with the options being "very well," "somewhat well," "not well," and "don't know." Surveyors inserted the phrases from the leftmost column of this table into the question when asking respondents. Variables are binary, with a 1 indicating "very well" and a 0 indicating all other choices.

SOURCE: BALS Employer Survey and BALS Household Survey (HIRE 2006).

A.1.c Problem-Solving

Skill	Employer skill set	Household Survey question
Prioritize tasks	Prioritize	11A
Gather information	Prioritize	11B
Sort and categorize information	Prioritize	11C
Identify work-related problems	Prioritize	11D
Identify potential solutions to problems	Evaluate	11E
Identify barriers to solutions	Evaluate	11F
Implement solutions	Leadership	11G
Evaluate results	Evaluate	11H
Use teamwork/collaborative problem-solving	Leadership	11I
Make decisions independently	Leadership	11J
Use leadership-oriented problem-solving	Leadership	11K

NOTE: Question 48 of the Employer Survey asks, "How well do you think you . . . ?" with the options being "very well," "somewhat well," "not well," and "don't know." Surveyors inserted the phrases from the leftmost column of this table into the question when asking respondents. Variables are binary, with a 1 indicating "very well" and a 0 indicating all other choices.

SOURCE: BALS Employer Survey and BALS Household Survey (HIRE 2006).

A.1.d Communication

Skill	Employer skill set	Household Survey question
Give spoken instructions in the workplace	Not used	10A
Choose words and manner of expression appropriate to the workplace	Coworkers	10B
Make and receive business phone calls	Customers	10C
Deal with customers	Customers	10D
Perceive verbal and nonverbal cues from others	Coworkers	10E
Explain products and services	Customers	10F
Handle complaints	Customers	10G
Interact with coworkers to accomplish a task	Coworkers	10H
Sell a product or service to a customer	Customers	10I

NOTE: Question 47 of the Employer Survey asks, "How well do you think you . . . (in English)?" with the options being "very well," "somewhat well," "not well," and "don't know." Surveyors inserted the phrases from the leftmost column of this table into the question when asking respondents. Variables are binary, with a 1 indicating "very well" and a 0 indicating all other choices.

SOURCE: BALS Employer Survey and BALS Household Survey (HIRE 2006).

A.1.e Computer Software

Skill	Employer skill set	Household Survey question
Word processing programs	Productivity Enhancers	13A
Spreadsheet programs	Productivity Enhancers	13B
Database software	Productivity Enhancers	13C
E-mail	Productivity Enhancers	13D
Internet browsers	Productivity Enhancers	13E
Web page design/authoring	Multimedia	13F
Multimedia authoring and editing software	Multimedia	13G
Graphics software	Multimedia	13H
Desktop publishing programs	Multimedia	13I
Financial inventory software	Financial	13J

NOTE: Question 50 of the Employer Survey asks, "How well can you use . . . ?" with the options being "very well," "somewhat well," "not well," and "don't know." Surveyors inserted the phrases from the leftmost column of this table into the question when asking respondents. Variables are binary, with a 1 indicating "very well" and a 0 indicating all other choices.

SOURCE: BALS Employer Survey and BALS Household Survey (HIRE 2006).

A.1.f Job Equipment

Skill	Employer skill set	Household Survey question
Telephone systems	Office	12A
Answering machines	Office	12B
Copiers	Office	12C
Fax machines	Office	12D
Macintosh or Apple computers	Not used	12E
Windows or DOS-based computers	Office	12F
Production machinery	Production	12G
Heavy equipment	Production	12H

NOTE: Question 49 of the Employer Survey asks, "How well can you operate . . . ?" with the options being "very well," "somewhat well," "not well," and "don't know." Surveyors inserted the phrases from the leftmost column of this table into the question when asking respondents. Variables are binary, with a 1 indicating "very well" and a 0 indicating all other choices.
SOURCE: BALS Employer Survey and BALS Household Survey (HIRE 2006).

Table A.2 Job Duties in BALS Jobs

SOC-O*NET occupational code and title	Job duties (as specified by BALS respondents)		
Management occupations			
13-1022.00 Wholesale and retail buyers, except farm products	• Run routes • Write checks • Deal with customers	• Assist with merchandise purchase • Communicate with faculty and students • Do special orders	
13-1079.99 Human resources, training, and labor relations specialists, all other	• Counsel participants • Work with welfare-to-work program	• Manage cases	
Community and social services			
21-1022.00 Medical and public health social workers	• Provide outreach referrals and information • Counsel program participants • Perform screening tests	• Interview clients • Assist in treatment and planning	
21-1093.00 Social and human service assistants	• Provide program services to clients		
Education, training, and library			
25-9041.00 Teacher assistants	• Assist in instruction • Tutor students • Monitor student drills, practices, and related activities	• Report progress of students • Provide help after school • Assist teachers in all activities and plans	
Art, design, entertainment, sports, and media			
27-1014.00 Multimedia artists and animators	• Create artwork for a show, computer games, etc.	• Use in-house software to integrate art and effect	

Code	Occupation	Tasks	
27-1029.99	Designers, all other	• Trace characters	• Perform computer-assisted design
27-4021.01	Professional photographers	• Label and take films • Track Polaroids	• Pack and unpack merchandise • Maintain studio
Health care practitioner and technical			
29-2071.00	Medical records and health information technicians	• Record medical information • File medical history	• Use computer programs
Health care support			
31-1011.00	Home health aides	• Provide personal care functions (grooming, feeding, bathing) • Housekeep and do housework (cooking, shopping, laundry)	• Give patients emotional support (e.g., chat with them) • Provide hospice care
31-1012.00	Nursing aides, orderlies, and attendants	• Provide personal care functions (bathing, feeding, dressing)	• Turn and reposition patients lying on bed • Communicate with patients
31-9092.00	Medical assistants	• Clean instruments • Assist technologist	• Prepare patients for exams • Monitor temperature of inventory • Report changes in patient's condition
31-9099.99	Health care support workers, all other	• Provide personal care support • Help patients with ambulation	• Provide personal care functions (grooming, feeding, dressing)
Protective services			
33-3012.00	Correctional officers and jailers	• Receive prisoners for detainment • Obtain information from prisoners	• Maintain discipline • Prevent escapes
33-3051.03	Police and sheriff's patrol officers	• Conduct patrols • Perform investigations	• Perform enforcement activities

(continued)

Table A.2 Job Duties in BALS Jobs (continued)

SOC-O*NET occupational code and title	Job duties (as specified by BALS respondents)
33-9011.00 Animal control workers	• Patrol assigned areas • Investigate work plants for the public • Investigate complaints regarding animal cruelty • Capture wild, stray, and unlicensed animals
33-9032.00 Security guards	• Check sites, doors, etc. • Observe and report any suspicious activity • Guard client's property • Control access (ID check)
Food preparation and serving–related	
35-2011.00 Cooks, fast food	• Make dough and pizza • Measure and mix ingredients • Clean food preparation area
35-2021.00 Food preparation workers	• Wash and chop food • Prepare vegetables and fruits to be used in dishes • Butcher poultry • Serve cook • Maintain the serving line
35-3021.00 Combined food preparation and serving workers, including fast food	• Use cash register • Clean and stock workstation • Prepare food • Take orders • Serve food
35-3031.00 Waiters and waitresses	• Take orders • Serve food • Clean and set up tables • Take care of customer payment
35-3041.00 Food servicers, nonrestaurant	• Check patients' diet and serve food accordingly • Pour and cover beverages • Set up food service carts and trays • Observe and control infection • Take care of procedures related to dietary department

35-9011.00   Dining room and cafeteria attendants and bartender helpers
- Clean and reset tables
- Serve food
- Wash dishes
- Cater

35-9021.00   Dishwashers
- Wash dishes, pots, and pans
- Maintain sanitation in the kitchen
- Clean equipment and floors
- Empty garbage

35-9031.00   Hosts and hostesses, restaurant, lounge, and coffee shop
- Answer phones
- Make reservations
- Serve and talk with sitting guests
- Check the cleanliness of restrooms

35-9099.99   Food preparation and serving-related workers, all other
- Prepare meal
- Serve portion
- Wash dishes
- Maintain diet

Building and grounds cleaning and maintenance

37-2011.00   Janitors and cleaners, except maids and housekeeping cleaners
- Clean assigned area/tools/equipment/materials
- Ensure security and alarm procedures are followed when entering/leaving
- Report hazardous conditions/items
- Follow infection control practice
- Empty waste receptacles

37-2012.00   Maids and housekeeping cleaners
- Clean rooms/floors/kitchen
- Water plants
- Serve meal in dining room
- Clean and remake beds

37-2019.99   Building cleaning workers, all other
- Clean facilities
- Use special cleaning equipment (such as wire brush)

37-2021.00   Pest control workers
- Identify pests
- Destroy and repel pests

37-3011.00   Landscaping and groundskeeping workers
- Irrigate plants
- Mow grass/trim greenery and hedge
- Prune brush
- Operate tractor and attachments
- Maintain tools and suppliers

Personal care and service

39-3093.00   Locker room, coatroom, and dressing room attendants
- Maintain inventories of clothing and accessories
- Assign locker space
- Serve customers with towels

(continued)

Table A.2 Job Duties in BALS Jobs (continued)

SOC-O*NET occupational code and title	Job duties (as specified by BALS respondents)
39-6011.00	Baggage handlers, porters, bellhops	• Park cars • Take guests' luggage out of car	• Carry guests' baggage to room • Arrange transportation
39-6012.00	Concierges	• Open gates • Load and unload groceries	• Watch for people coming and leaving
39-9011.00	Child care workers	• Supervise child or children's group before/after school	• Supervise homework/study • Supervise playground
39-9021.00	Personal and home care aides	• Cook • Housekeep	• Do laundry • Sit with elders
39-9031.00	Fitness trainers and aerobics instructors	• Write exercise program for members	• Instruct members
39-9032.00	Recreation workers	• Assist program directors • Implement recreation programs	• Perform recreational activities
39-3091.00	Amusement and recreation assistants	• Load equipment (e.g., trap houses for skeet shooting)	• Maintain/store equipment and tools • Clean up equipment and tools
Sales and related			
41-2011.00	Cashiers	• Scan/bag items • Use cash register	• Handle customer payments • Prepare the sales floor
41-2021.00	Counter and rental clerks	• Take orders • Stock suppliers • Serve customers	• Operate register equipment and tools • Receive payments • Answer phones and distribute mail
41-2031.00	Retail salespersons	• Provide products and services • Handle complaints • Use cash register	• Maintain stores (stock levels, appearance, visual merchandising)

Code	Occupation	Duties
41-4012.00	Sales representatives, wholesale, and manufacturing, except technical and scientific products	• Set up displays (on-premise & off-premise) • Reorder products for maintaining stock • Serve customers
41-9022.00	Real estate agents	• Sell or lease properties • Find property sellers and buyers and bridge them • Show properties • Assist customers with paperwork of application/contract
41-9041.00	Telemarketers	• Sell products on phone • Handle customer complaints • Deal with graph department

Office and administrative support

Code	Occupation	Duties
43-2021.00	Telephone operators	• Answer (main telephone line) and transfer calls • Handle mail (incoming and outgoing)
43-3021.03	Billing, posting, and calculating machine operators	• Record financial data daily • Provide daily cash report • Book accounts receivable and collect • Research credit balances on accounts • Assist customers with billing inquiries • Operate machines
43-3031.00	Bookkeeping, accounting, and auditing clerks	• Book accounting records (e.g., accounts payable, expenses) • Check approval and necessary documents • Watch bank deposits closely • Schedule payments • Consolidate accounts • Implement monthly/yearly closing
43-3051.00	Payroll and timekeeping clerks	• Process payroll • Deliver payrolls
43-3071.00	Tellers	• Handle cash transactions • Assist customers with opening new accounts • Communicate with clients • Sell bank products
43-4051.02	Customer service representatives	• Serve customers (mostly on phone) • Refill orders • Enter data for information and details • Provide technical service

Table A.2 Job Duties in BALS Jobs (continued)

SOC-O*NET occupational code and title	Job duties (as specified by BALS respondents)
43-4071.00 File clerks	• Enter data • File (soft copy and hard copy)	• Sort files
43-4081.00 Hotel, motel, and reservation desk clerks	• Answer phones • Take reservations	• Check in guests
43-4111.00 Interviewers, except eligibility and loan	• Poll public on opinions • Conduct market research surveys	• Operate computer (such as CATI)
43-4121.00 Library assistants, clerical	• Shelve books/periodical articles • Serve at the circulation desk	• Register library patrons • Enter information via computer and serve patrons with it
43-4131.00 Loan interviewers and clerks	• Interview loan applicants to elicit information • Investigate applicants' backgrounds	• Perform office clerical work (filing, phone answering, etc.)
43-4151.00 Order clerks	• Receive and process incoming orders	
43-4171.00 Receptionists and information clerks	• Greet and direct visitors • Provide information	• Answer multiline phone system and transfer calls • Prepare and distribute mail
43-5031.00 Police, fire, and ambulance dispatchers	• Receive 911 calls and transfer to appropriate parties • Dispatch police units	• Handle inquiries and complaints from public • Operate multichannel radio system
43-5032.00 Dispatchers, except police, fire, and ambulance	• Take customer phone calls • Call the closest available cab	• Document appointments and phone calls from cabs
43-5061.00 Production, planning, and expediting clerks	• Pull out right products according to orders	• Restock when needed

43-5081.03   Stock clerks and order fillers
- Merchandise stocks
- Load and unload stocks
- Sign for receipt of supplies
- Restock supplies
- Pull and package parts

43-6013.00   Medical secretaries
- Schedule appointments
- Answer phones
- Assist physicians and nurses

43-6014.00   Secretaries, except legal, medical, and executive
- Answer phones
- Type up contracts and other paperwork

43-9021.00   Data entry keyers
- Enter data
- Assist with charts (preparation, filling out, managing)
- Verify information provided outside the agency

43-9051.01   Mail clerks, except mail machine operators and postal service
- Handle incoming and outgoing mail
- Prepare bulk mail for post office
- Assist all staff with mailing materials and information
- Assist visitors

43-9061.00   Office clerks, general
- Answer phones
- Perform basic bookkeeping
- Enter data
- Provide reception
- Process mail
- Provide administrative support (e.g., copying, printing)

43-9071.01   Office machine operators, except computer
- Provide high volume copy
- Check working quality of machine
- Pull information off microfilm/copy

43-9199.99   Office and administrative support workers, all other
- Understand financial bookkeeping
- Operate computer
- Interact with public

Farming, fishing, and forestry

45-2041.00   Graders and sorters, agricultural products
- Sort by size, quality, domestic/export
- Sort broken items and debris out of cutter
- Grade plants

(continued)

Table A.2 Job Duties in BALS Jobs (continued)

SOC-O*NET occupational code and title		Job duties (as specified by BALS respondents)
Construction and extraction		
47-2031.01	Carpenters	• Use screwdrivers, hammers, etc. • Make items out of wood
47-2061.00	Construction laborers	• Repair pallets; use hammer, nails, nail gun • Clean up site • Load/unload docks
47-2071.00	Paving, surfacing, and tamping equipment operators	• Dig ditches, demolition • Haul debris and materials • Stock Sheetrock • Break and remove pavements
47-2152.03	Pipelaying fitters	• Lay pipe • Work on assembly chart
47-3012.00	Helpers, carpenters	• Frame • Cut boards
47-4051.00	Highway maintenance workers	• Maintain safety of roads • Operate specified vehicles
47-4071.00	Septic tank servicers and sewer pipe cleaners	• Clean sewers • Operate specified vehicles
Installation, maintenance, and repair		
49-2022.03	Communication equipment mechanics	• Pull and correct cables • Repair communication equipment
49-3011.00	Aircraft mechanics and service technicians	• Replace aircraft accessories • Make necessary adjustments and settings • Test equipment
49-3021.00	Automotive body and related repairers	• Repair dents • Prime and paint body • Weld
49-3022.00	Automotive glass installers and repairers	• Drive onsite • Install glass

49-3023.00	Automotive service technicians and mechanics	• Repair auto parts (such as transmission)	• Maintain autos
49-9042.00	Maintenance and repair workers, general	• Maintain houses • Repair plumbing, appliances, electrical wiring	• Mow, trim, and paint • Maintain yards
49-9043.00	Maintenance workers, machinery	• Fix machines on the line • Clean machines • Polish parts	• Inspect the operation of machines • Document maintenance issues

Production

51-1011.00	First-line supervisor/manager of production and operating workers	• Manage crew • Manage business flow	• Manage inventory
51-2099.99	Assemblers and fabricators, all other	• Assemble • Power-sand and inspect cabinets • Wire lighting	• Follow blueprint • Operate machines and equipment
51-3021.00	Butchers and meat cutters	• Cut meat • Slaughter or dress meat for market	• Follow safety instructions
51-4121.02	Welders and cutters	• Weld, cut, and blowtorch	• Weld
51-6011.03	Laundry and dry-cleaning machine operators and tenders, except pressing	• Wash or dry-clean valuable clothes (such as tuxedo)	• Operate/tend washing or dry-cleaning machines • Fold clothes
51-6031.01	Sewing machine operators	• Sew garments	
51-6041.00	Shoe and leather workers and repairers	• Repair shoes with hands or machine • Sew, do workbench repair, and sand	• Finish work
51-7041.02	Sawing machine setters, operators, and wood tenders	• Place foam on saw table • Perform programmed cuts	• Move pieces onto conveyor

(continued)

156

Table A.2 Job Duties in BALS Jobs (continued)

SOC-O*NET occupational code and title	Job duties (as specified by BALS respondents)
51-9023.00 Mixing and blending machine setters, operators, and tenders	• Service operating lines • Assist with anything needed on site
51-9061.01 Inspectors, testers, sorters, samplers, and weighers	• Inspect the setup of the line • Follow quality assurance direction • Inspect PET (polyethylene therephthalate) bottles and perform tests on them • Monitor for defects and report • Weigh samples
51-9111.00 Packing and filling machine operators and tenders	• Stack newspapers • Load bundles of newspapers
51-9131.03 Photographic hand developers	• Check negative vs. positive prints • Crop pictures • Check color and density • Trim photos
51-9192.02 Cleaning, washing, and metal pickling equipment operators and tenders	• Support production lines • Clean floors • Dump tubs
51-9198.01 Production laborers	• Monitor performance of machines • Follow safety processes • Assemble components • Maintain quality levels demanded • Pack products • Operate machinery
51-9198.02 Production helpers	• Clean machine • Help other employees at higher skill level • Assist with operation of machinery • Pack products
51-9199.99 Production workers, all others	• Stack T-shirts • Fold clothes and put into boxes

Transportation and material moving

Code	Title	Duties
53-3021.00	Bus drivers, transit and intercity	• Transport passengers in a safe manner
53-3032.01	Truck drivers, heavy and tractor-trailer	• Drive trucks for towing vehicles • Read maps • Fill out forms when needed
53-3033.00	Truck drivers, light or delivery services	• Deliver goods • Load/unload trucks • Perform multiple pickups
53-6021.00	Parking lot attendants	• Keep lots clean • Ensure safety of lot • Provide customer services on demand
53-7051.00	Industrial truck and tractor operator	• Drive tractor • Operate forklift
53-7061.00	Cleaners of vehicles and equipment wash	• Clean cars • Pick up/deliver cars to customers
53-7062.03	Freight, stock, and material movers, hand	• Unload/load trucks and trailers • Maintain stock supply levels • Verify inbound merchandise for accuracy • Read and fulfill instructions • Move boxes/material to right location
53-7064.00	Packers and packagers, hand	• Pack goods/groceries into boxes/bags • Label product • Wrap packages

Military-specific

Code	Title	Duties
55-3016.00	Infantry	• Vary according to department

NOTE: The SOC-O*NET system classifies about 1,000 occupations into categories based on common characteristics. The codes and titles used to access information about each occupation are used to organize information in this table. The 405 employers were each asked for a job title and to list the job duties of the low-skilled position. The positions were coded using SOC-O*NET categories, and duties for the positions were consolidated and summarized within each SOC-O*NET category.
SOURCE: BALS Employer Survey (HIRE 2006).

Table A.3 Skills Needed in Low-Skilled Jobs: Factor Analysis of O*NET Data

	English communication	Mechanical skills	Physical abilities		Math	Problem-solving	Communality
			Large motor	Small motor			
Knowledge							
Mechanical	-0.147	**0.805**	0.446	0.084	0.025	0.028	0.877
Mathematics	0.200	0.186	-0.085	0.065	**0.893**	0.004	0.884
Skills							
Operation and control	-0.104	**0.904**	0.019	0.148	0.083	0.151	0.880
Equipment selection	-0.133	**0.679**	0.261	0.320	0.158	-0.011	0.674
Mathematics	0.200	0.186	0.085	0.065	**0.893**	0.004	0.884
Reading comprehension	**0.733**	0.087	-0.289	0.033	0.361	-0.003	0.760
Monitoring	0.446	0.118	-0.169	0.236	0.028	0.253	0.363
Active listening	**0.850**	-0.319	-0.022	-0.144	-0.039	0.012	0.847
Writing	**0.750**	0.049	-0.140	0.020	0.432	0.010	0.772
Operation monitoring	-0.088	**0.895**	-0.001	0.173	0.144	0.177	0.891
Quality control analysis	-0.095	**0.753**	-0.042	0.318	0.358	0.131	0.824
Equipment maintenance	-0.098	**0.839**	0.288	0.098	0.130	0.014	0.823
Speaking	**0.834**	-0.256	-0.059	-0.185	0.031	0.114	0.813
Abilities							
Near vision	0.151	0.219	-0.114	**0.728**	0.133	0.291	0.715
Information ordering	0.173	0.358	0.394	**0.584**	0.281	0.090	0.741
Manual dexterity	-0.351	0.250	**0.520**	**0.593**	0.090	0.096	0.825
Problem sensitivity	0.216	0.293	0.110	-0.057	0.402	**0.644**	0.725

	Factor 1	Factor 2	Factor 3	Factor 4	Factor 5	Factor 6	h^2
Wrist-finger speed	0.003	0.059	0.178	**0.779**	-0.041	-0.116	0.658
Written comprehension	**0.682**	0.085	-0.223	0.134	0.434	0.137	0.748
Oral comprehension	**0.822**	-0.222	0.079	-0.104	0.081	0.164	0.775
Extent of flexibility	-0.059	0.195	**0.844**	0.290	-0.025	0.042	0.840
Arm-hand scale	-0.374	0.196	0.306	**0.677**	0.080	0.189	0.773
Static strength	-0.046	0.187	**0.882**	0.047	-0.041	0.031	0.820
Control precision	-0.090	**0.743**	0.252	0.413	-0.005	0.172	0.824
Multilimb coordination	-0.150	0.426	**0.659**	0.230	-0.160	0.222	0.767
Number facility	0.404	0.061	0.020	0.305	**0.599**	0.203	0.661
Trunk strength	-0.042	0.101	**0.865**	0.249	-0.025	-0.068	0.827
Finger dexterity	-0.193	0.233	0.118	**0.829**	0.053	0.050	0.797
Selective attention	0.277	0.084	0.007	0.358	0.072	**0.746**	0.774
Oral expression	**0.829**	-0.256	0.031	-0.163	0.069	0.220	0.833
Visualization	-0.074	0.342	0.388	**0.625**	0.179	0.187	0.730
Written expression	**0.666**	0.072	-0.130	0.066	**0.500**	0.240	0.777
Deductive reasoning	0.264	0.270	0.220	0.220	0.470	0.431	0.645
Time sharing	0.486	0.016	0.255	0.177	0.088	**0.661**	0.777
Perceptual speed	0.152	0.282	0.116	**0.643**	0.147	0.329	0.660
Reaction time	0.159	0.349	0.412	0.142	-0.212	**0.606**	0.749
Speed of limb movement	-0.244	0.119	**0.679**	0.398	-0.131	0.333	0.821
Stamina	-0.074	0.013	**0.887**	-0.081	-0.016	0.130	0.815
Variance explained by factor	6.245	6.039	5.596	5.093	3.578	2.814	29.366
Percent variance explained	16.4	15.9	14.7	13.4	9.4	7.4	77.3

(continued)

160

Table A.3 Skills Needed in Low-Skilled Jobs: Factor Analysis of O*NET Data (continued)

N	135

NOTE: Numbers in the first through sixth numeric columns are the rotated factor loadings computed using an oblique (nonorthogonal) rotation. Variables used in the factor analysis indicate the level of intensity, measured on a scale from 1 (lowest) to 7 (highest), of the skills used in at least 50 percent of the Job Zone 1 jobs. (See text Table 1.2.) The communality reflects the proportion of the variation of each variable involved in the pattern (the sum of the squared factor loadings). The total variance is the sum of the communalities divided by the number of variables and tells the percentage of the variation among all the variables that is explained by the factor patterns. Boldface numbers show factor loadings greater than or equal to 0.5.

SOURCE: O*NET Job Zone 1 (O*NET 2006c).

Table A.4 Skills Needed in Low-Skilled Jobs: Factor Analysis of BALS Data

	Communication and problem-solving	Large motor	Mechanical	Small motor	Math	Assembly	Communality
Knowledge							
Mechanical	-0.132	**0.585**	**0.646**	0.132	0.071	0.019	0.799
Mathematics	0.401	-0.266	-0.018	0.056	**0.815**	-0.029	0.901
Skills							
Operation and control	-0.099	0.322	**0.809**	0.005	0.061	0.171	0.801
Equipment selection	0.076	-0.023	**0.805**	0.185	-0.167	-0.126	0.732
Mathematics	0.401	-0.266	-0.018	0.056	**0.815**	-0.029	0.901
Reading comprehension	**0.712**	-0.542	-0.094	-0.005	0.258	-0.170	0.906
Monitoring	**0.724**	-0.392	0.172	0.050	0.012	-0.102	0.720
Active listening	**0.783**	-0.419	-0.158	-0.129	0.097	-0.233	0.894
Writing	**0.763**	-0.396	-0.115	-0.024	0.204	-0.199	0.834
Operation monitoring	-0.093	0.330	**0.838**	0.071	-0.046	0.230	0.879
Quality control analysis	0.180	-0.041	**0.826**	0.210	0.130	0.107	0.789
Equipment maintenance	-0.114	0.383	**0.810**	0.135	-0.036	-0.078	0.841
Speaking	**0.822**	-0.306	-0.139	-0.130	0.165	-0.234	0.887
Abilities							
Near vision	**0.694**	-0.213	0.007	0.381	0.286	0.283	0.834
Information ordering	0.437	0.333	0.321	0.347	0.245	0.452	0.790
Manual dexterity	-0.275	0.446	0.287	**0.704**	-0.034	0.130	0.871
Problem sensitivity	**0.822**	-0.042	0.148	0.122	0.147	-0.099	0.745

(continued)

Table A.4 Skills Needed in Low-Skilled Jobs: Factor Analysis of BALS Data (continued)

	Communication and problem-solving	Large motor	Mechanical	Small motor	Math	Assembly	Communality
Wrist-finger speed	−0.214	0.062	0.183	0.216	−0.046	**0.797**	0.768
Written comprehension	**0.744**	−0.304	0.019	−0.146	0.360	0.101	0.807
Oral comprehension	**0.820**	−0.073	−0.108	−0.260	0.148	−0.081	0.785
Extent of flexibility	−0.241	**0.884**	0.155	0.235	0.034	0.036	0.921
Arm-hand scale	0.034	0.366	0.213	**0.789**	−0.050	0.113	0.818
Static strength	−0.208	**0.807**	0.308	0.085	−0.214	−0.017	0.843
Control precision	0.024	0.350	**0.675**	0.298	−0.092	0.312	0.773
Multilimb coordination	−0.156	**0.751**	0.376	0.187	−0.238	−0.015	0.821
Number facility	**0.568**	−0.044	−0.047	0.022	**0.539**	**0.501**	0.869
Trunk strength	−0.302	**0.891**	0.033	0.126	0.012	0.009	0.903
Finger dexterity	0.043	0.053	0.207	**0.890**	0.074	0.148	0.867
Selective attention	**0.828**	0.005	0.098	0.238	−0.101	0.169	0.791
Oral expression	**0.891**	−0.113	−0.218	−0.108	0.156	−0.074	0.895
Visualization	0.248	0.498	0.324	**0.527**	0.090	−0.141	0.720
Written expression	**0.855**	−0.231	−0.032	−0.121	0.242	0.253	0.923
Deductive reasoning	**0.805**	−0.174	0.060	0.232	0.341	−0.140	0.872
Time sharing	**0.866**	0.110	0.016	0.083	−0.127	0.182	0.818
Perceptual speed	**0.587**	0.034	0.157	0.442	0.164	0.418	0.767
Reaction time	0.017	**0.611**	0.371	0.049	−0.290	0.423	0.778

Speed of limb movement	−0.225	**0.748**	0.245	0.230	−0.247	0.292	0.870
Stamina	−0.311	**0.824**	0.203	0.032	−0.265	−0.034	0.889
Variance explained by factor	10.711	7.199	5.348	3.365	2.736	2.264	31.623
Percent variance explained	28.2	18.9	14.1	8.9	7.2	6.0	83.2
N				399			

NOTE: Numbers in the first through sixth numeric columns are the rotated factor loadings computed using an oblique (nonorthogonal) rotation as applied to the O*NET-defined skills that are linked to BALS jobs through the SOC-O*NET code. Boldface numbers show factor loadings greater than or equal to 0.5. O*NET did not contain skills information for six occupations in the BALS data set.

SOURCE: BALS Employer Survey (HIRE 2006).

Table A.5 Definition of Variables Used in the Analysis of Occupational Wages

Variable	Definition
Dependent variables	
Log wage	Log of starting hourly rate of pay in position (average if the position pays a range).
Reach $15/hr.	A 0/1 binary variable with 1 indicating that the job has the potential to pay (or pays) $15 an hour.
Independent variables	
Skills	
Simple English	The factor score from a factor analysis of the BALS English reading and writing skills needed in the position. Skills loading high include reading written instructions, labels, schedules, and journals; reading general memos, letters, and forms; reading technical materials; writing simple sentences and paragraphs; and completing forms, logs, charges, or labels.
Complex English	The factor score from a factor analysis of the BALS English reading and writing skills needed in the position. Skills loading high include using correct spelling, grammar, and style; proofreading; and writing complex or creative materials or reports.
Applied math	The factor score from a factor analysis of the BALS math skills needed in the position. Skills loading high include making change, calculating discounts and markups of the selling price, and using equipment (e.g., a calculator or a business machine).
Algebra	The factor score from a factor analysis of the BALS math skills needed in the position. Skills loading high include using ratios, fractions, decimals, or percentages; estimating or rounding off numbers; solving simple equations; and interpreting data from graphs, tables, or charts.
Measurement	The factor score from a factor analysis of the BALS math skills needed in the position. Skills loading high include using simple measurements and measurement instruments.
Prioritizing	The factor score from a factor analysis of the BALS problem-solving skills needed in the position. Skills loading high include prioritizing tasks, gathering information, sorting and categorizing information, and identifying work-related problems.

Evaluating	The factor score from a factor analysis of the BALS problem-solving skills needed in the position. Skills loading high include identifying potential solutions to problems, identifying barriers to solutions, and evaluating results.
Leadership	The factor score from a factor analysis of BALS problem-solving skills needed in the position. Skills loading high include applying solutions to problems, working in teams, making decisions independently, and providing leadership in problem-solving.
Customers	The factor score from a factor analysis of the BALS communication skills needed in the position. Skills loading high include making and receiving business phone calls, dealing with customers, explaining products and services, handling complaints, and selling a product or service to a customer.
Coworkers	The factor score from a factor analysis of the BALS communication skills needed in the position. Skills loading high include choosing words and manner of expression appropriate to the workplace, picking up on verbal and nonverbal cues from others, and interacting with coworkers to accomplish a task.
Productivity enhancers	The factor score from a factor analysis of the BALS software/program skills needed in the position. Skills loading high include the ability to use word processing programs, spreadsheet programs, database software, e-mail, and Internet browsers.
Multimedia software	The factor score from a factor analysis of the BALS software/program skills needed in the position. Skills loading high include the ability to use Web page design/authoring programs, multimedia authoring and editing software, graphics software, and desktop publishing programs.
Financial software	The factor score from a factor analysis of the BALS software/program skills needed in the position. Skills loading high include the ability to use financial inventory software.
Office equipment	The factor score from a factor analysis of the BALS equipment skills needed in the position. Skills loading high include the ability to operate telephone systems (multiple lines), telephone answering machines, copiers, fax machines, and DOS-based computers.
Production equipment	The factor score from a factor analysis of the BALS equipment skills needed in the position. Skills loading high include the ability to operate production machinery and heavy equipment (e.g., forklifts, cranes).

(continued)

Table A.5 Definition of Variables used in the Analysis of Occupational Wages (continued)

Variable	Definition
Communication and problem-solving	The factor score from a factor analysis of BALS occupations linked to O*NET through the SOC-O*NET code. Skills loading high include reading comprehension, monitoring, active listening, writing, speaking, near vision, problem sensitivity, written and oral comprehension, number facility, selective attention, oral and written expression, deductive reasoning, time sharing, and perceptual speed.
Math	The factor score from a factor analysis of BALS occupations linked to O*NET through the SOC-O*NET code. Skills loading high include mathematics knowledge and skill, and number facility.
Mechanical	The factor score from a factor analysis of BALS occupations linked to O*NET through the SOC-O*NET code. Skills loading high include mechanical, operation and control, equipment selection, operation monitoring, quality control analysis, equipment maintenance, and control precision.
Large motor	The factor score from a factor analysis of BALS occupations linked to O*NET through the SOC-O*NET code. Skills loading high include mechanical, extent flexibility, static strength, multilimb coordination, trunk strength, speed of limb movement, and stamina.
Small motor	The factor score from a factor analysis of BALS occupations linked to O*NET through the SOC-O*NET code. Skills loading high include manual dexterity, arm-hand scale, finger dexterity, and visualization.
Assembly	The factor score from a factor analysis of BALS occupations linked to O*NET through the SOC-O*NET code. Skills loading high include wrist-finger speed and number facility.
Institutional	
Small firm	A 0/1 binary variable, with 1 indicating a small (50 or fewer employees) firm.
Large firm	A 0/1 binary variable, with 1 indicating a large (300 or more employees) firm.
Service industry	A 0/1 binary variable, with 1 indicating a firm in the service sector (1987 Standard Industrial Classification [SIC] of 70–72, 74–79, 81, 83–86, or 88–89).

Manufacturing industry	A 0/1 binary variable, with 1 indicating a firm in the manufacturing sector (1987 SIC of 20-40).
Retail trade industry	A 0/1 binary variable, with 1 indicating a firm in the education or retail sector (1987 SIC of 52–60).
Business service industry	A 0/1 binary variable, with 1 indicating a firm in the business service sector (1987 SIC of 73 or 87, which includes engineering, accounting, research, management, and related services, such as business services).
Ed and med industry	A 0/1 binary variable, with 1 indicating a firm in the education or medical sector (1987 SIC of 80 or 82).
Union	A 0/1 binary variable, with 1 indicating that the incumbent in the position is represented by a union.
Labor market	
Unemployment rate	County unemployment rate during the month of surveying.

Table A.6 Types of Entry-Level Jobs and Promotions Available

Examples of entry-level jobs	Typical promotion	Other promotional opportunities
Business and financial operations		
Asst. buyer, buyback operator	Manager (100.0%)	
Resource specialist		
Community and social services		
Community health worker	None	Community health specialist
Peer advisor		Peer counselor
Art, design, entertainment, sports, and media		
Multimedia artist	None	Producer
Junior designer		Designer
Photo assistant		Photographer
Education, training, and library		
Assistant instructor	Office clerk (100.0%)	
Instruction assistant/aide		
Healthcare practitioner and technical		
Medical record technician	None	Numerous possibilities
Health care support		
Health worker	Lead/supervisor (40.0%)	Clerical/receptionist
Home health aid		Certified nursing
Hospital services tech. I		Lab assistant II
Lab assistant		Recreation assistant
Medical assistant		Rehabilitation asst.
Nursing assistant not certified		
Protective service		
Animal control	Site/field supervisor (80.0%)	Patrol controller
Correctional officer trainee		Correctional officer
Deputy sheriff trainee		Deputy sheriff
Security guard/officer		Reception desk
		Sergeant
		Site supervisor
Food preparation and serving–related		
Assistant host	Cook (44.0%)	Bus person
Bus boy (person)	Leader/supervisor (36.0%)	Crew trainer
Cashier		Security guard
Cook, line cook, prep cook		
Crew members		
Custodian		

Table A.6 (continued)

Examples of entry-level jobs	Typical promotion	Other promotional opportunities
Building and grounds cleaning and maintenance		
Aid	Lead/supervisor/	Expert climbing tree
Apprentice	foreman (32.1%)	Mechanic
Cleaning/housekeeper	Janitor/custodian (25.0%)	Housekeeper
Custodian/janitor	Personal asst. (17.9%)	Inspector
Environmental services	Housekeeper (14.3%)	Park and facility
Gardener		maintenance
General laborer		Personal assistant
Greenskeeper		
Ground crew/worker		
Maintenance position		
Landscape crew/gardener		
Utilities person		
Personal care and service		
Bell person	None	Bell captain
Cart driver		Care giver
Companion		Personal trainer
Day care worker		Program director
Doorperson		Recreation leader
Recreation leader		Teacher's aide
Skeet set scorer		
Sports desk		
Valet		
Weight trainer		
Sales and related		
Cashier	Lead/supervisor/manager/	Customer service
Checkers	assistant manager (51.9%)	Floor rep
Clerk, registry, or sales		Host
Customer representative		Level II
Front counter		Merchandising
General packaging/counter		Production personnel
Leasing consultant		Telemarketing
Level 1		
Merchandiser		
Relief manager		
Sales		
Sales assistant/associate		
Stock		
Service agent		

(continued)

Table A.6 Types of Entry-Level Jobs and Promotions Available (continued)

Examples of entry-level jobs	Typical promotion	Other promotional opportunities
Office and administrative support		
Accounts payable	Administrative assistant,	10-key operator
Administrative support assistant	secretary, office manager (40.6%)	Accounting, billing, payroll Asst. housekeeper
Administrator I	Management/supervisor/	Cashier
Appointment setter	lead (17.9%)	Clerk (all kinds)
Associate	Customer service/	Coder
Cashier	reservations/front desk	Controller assistant
Clerical/clerical support	(8.5%)	Data entry
Clerk (all types)		Dental assistant
Computer dispatcher		Department assistant II
Coordinator		Equipment operator
Copy operator/puller		Fulfillment specialist
Customer service		Human resources assistant
Data entry/processing		Item processing
Department assistant		Library clerk II
File clerk		License registration
Financial representative III		examiner
Finisher		Marketing assistant
Field representative		Mortuary assistant
Front desk		Office assistant
General warehouse associate		Office technician
Ground person		Police tele-communicator II
Guest service representative		Sales
High school hub		Secretary
Library assistant		Senior proof operator
Loan processor		Small format/printing/
Mail order packing		customer printer
Marketing assistant		Staff assistant
Night person		Tech 2 lead position
Order processor/selector		Technical
Pbx/telephone operator		administrator
Police tele-communicator I		
Proof operator (10-key)		
Receptionist		
Record center specialist		
Right auditor		
Secretary		
Telephone interviewer		
Teller		

Table A.6 (continued)

Examples of entry-level jobs	Typical promotion	Other promotional opportunities
Farming, fishing, and forestry		
Asparagus/cucumber/ tomato sorter	None	Floor leader Prep/cleanup
Construction and extraction		
Carpentry worker	None	Carpenter
Collection system worker I		Maintenance lead worker Collection system worker II
General construction worker		
Highway maintenance worker		
Laborer		
Pipe fabricator		
Installation, maintenance and repair		
Aircraft mechanic level 5	Technician (42.9%)	Assistant manager
Body man apprentice	Mechanic (28.6%)	Body man
Cable technician		Mechanic
Installer		Technician
Mechanic trainee		
Technician		
Production		
Assembler	Management/lead/	Concrete finisher
Attendant	supervisor (30.2%)	Crew position
Butcher	Machine operator/	Data collector/operator/
General laborer/laborer	mechanic (20.9%)	handler
Laundry attendant		Editor/producer
Machine operator/ machiner		Fabricator
Manual laborer		Grade 2
Mill hand		Helper
Misc. helper		Middle butchering
Newspaper packaging trainees		Polisher
Photo checker		QA coordinator
Production/production worker		Rental agent
Quality assurance/ inspector		Screen painter
Sanitor		Shipping, packaging, checker, loader
Seamstress		Tester position
Shift leader		Trade
Shoe repairman/helper		Wire II
Welder		

(continued)

Table A.6 Types of Entry-Level Jobs and Promotions Available (continued)

Examples of entry-level jobs	Typical promotion	Other promotional opportunities
Transportation and material moving		
Assembly/production worker	Manager, lead, supervisor (29.0%)	Cashier
Bagger	Warehouse (23.7%)	Counter
Car washer	Counter/sales/cashier/ clerk (15.8%)	Daily bakery
Cart person		Detailer
Dock worker	Machine operator/ mechanic (10.5%)	Driver
Driver		Operational or technical
Forklift operator		Pro shop assistant
Furniture mover		Shipping
General laborer		
Lot attendant		
Material handler		
Packer		
Transit operator		
Warehouse		
Military specific		
Military entry-level position I	None	Military entry-level position II

NOTE: Job titles under the column headings "Examples of entry-level jobs," "Typical promotion," and "Other promotional opportunities" are the actual titles given for the position in the entry-level job and in the position above entry level (for advancement). The percentage of titles with advancement (middle column) is the percentage of entry-level positions having the potential for advancement without obtaining a four-year college degree. Titles under the "Typical promotion" category are job titles with at least two positions and at least 10 percent of titles leading to them for advancement.

SOURCE: BALS Employer Survey (HIRE 2006).

References

Akerlof, George A. 1980. "A Theory of Social Customs, of Which Unemployment May Be One Consequence." *Quarterly Journal of Economics* 94(4): 749–775.

Akerlof, George A., and Janet L. Yellen. 1986. *Efficiency Wage Models of the Labor Market*. Cambridge: Cambridge University Press.

Andersson, Fredrik, Harry J. Holzer, and Julia I. Lane. 2005. *Moving Up or Moving On: Who Advances in the Low-Wage Labor Market?* New York: Russell Sage Foundation.

Autor, David H., Lawrence F. Katz, and Alan B. Krueger. 1998. "Computing Inequality: Have Computers Changed the Labor Market?" *Quarterly Journal of Economics* 113(4): 1169–1213.

Autor, David H., Frank Levy, and Richard J. Murnane. 2003. "The Skill Content of Recent Technological Change: An Empirical Exploration." *Quarterly Journal of Economics* 118(4): 1279–1333.

Avery, Richard D., and Robert H. Faley. 1988. *Fairness in Selecting Employees*. Reading, MA: Addison-Wesley.

Baker, George P., Michael Gibbs, and Bengt Holmstrom. 1994. "The Internal Economics of the Firm: Evidence from Personnel Data." *Quarterly Journal of Economics* 109(4): 881–919.

Baker, George P., Michael C. Jensen, and Kevin J. Murphy. 1988. "Compensation and Incentives: Practice vs. Theory." *Journal of Finance* 43(3): 593–616.

Baron, James N., Alison Davis-Blake, and William T. Bielby. 1986. "The Structure of Opportunity: How Promotion Ladders Vary within and among Organizations." *Administrative Science Quarterly* 31(2): 248–273.

Bartel, Ann P., and Frank R. Lichtenberg. 1987. "The Comparative Advantage of Educated Workers in Implementing New Technology." *Review of Economics and Statistics* 69(1): 1–11.

Bartik, Timothy J. 2001. *Jobs for the Poor: Can Labor Demand Policies Help?* New York: Russell Sage Foundation.

Becker, Brian E., and Stephen M. Hills. 1980. "Teenage Unemployment: Some Evidence of the Long-Run Effects on Wages." *Journal of Human Resources* 15(3): 295–312.

———. 1983. "The Long-Run Effects of Job Changes and Unemployment among Male Teenagers." *Journal of Human Resources* 18(2): 197–212.

Benhabib, Jess, and Clive Bull. 1983. "Job Search: The Choice of Intensity." *Journal of Political Economy* 91(5): 747–764.

Bernhardt, Annette, Martina Morris, Mark S. Handcock, and Marc A. Scott. 2001. *Divergent Paths: Economic Mobility in the New American Labor*

Market. New York: Russell Sage Foundation.

Bils, David B. 1988. "Educational Credentials and Hiring Decisions: What Employers Look For in New Employees." *Research in Social Stratification and Mobility* 7(1): 71–97.

―――. 1999. "Labor Market Information and Selection in a Local Restaurant Industry: The Tenuous Balance between Rewards, Commitments, and Costs." *Sociological Forum* 14(4): 583–607.

Blackburn, McKinley L., David E. Bloom, and Richard B. Freeman. 1990. "The Declining Economic Position of Less Skilled American Men." In *A Future of Lousy Jobs? The Changing Structure of U.S. Wages,* Gary Burtless, ed. Washington, DC: Brookings Institution Press, pp. 31–76.

Blackburn, McKinley L., and David Neumark. 1993. "Omitted-Ability Bias and the Increase in the Return to Schooling." *Journal of Labor Economics* 11(3): 521–544.

Bloom, Howard S., Larry L. Orr, George Cave, Stephen H. Bell, Fred Doolittle, and Winston Lin. 1994. *The National JTPA Study. Overview: Impacts, Benefits, and Costs of Title II-A.* Bethesda, MD: Abt Associates.

Boesel, David, and Eric Fredland. 1999. *College for All? Is There Too Much Emphasis on Getting a 4-Year College Degree?* Washington, DC: U.S. Department of Education.

Bound, John, and Harry J. Holzer. 1993. "Industrial Shifts, Skills Levels, and the Labor Market for White and Black Males." *Review of Economics and Statistics* 75(3): 387–396.

Bowles, Samuel. 1985. "The Production Process in a Competitive Economy: Walrasian, Neo-Hobbesian, and Marxian Models." *American Economic Review* 75(1): 16–36.

Bulow, Jeremy I., and Lawrence H. Summers. 1986. "A Theory of Dual Labor Markets with Application to Industrial Policy, Discrimination, and Keynesian Unemployment." *Journal of Labor Economics* 4(3): 376–414.

Bureau of Labor Statistics (BLS). 2002a. "Occupational Employment and Wages, 2001." News release, November 6, 2002. Washington, DC: BLS. ftp://ftp.bls.gov/pub/news.release/history/ocwage.11062002.news (accessed May 15, 2006).

―――. 2002b. *NLS: The National Longitudinal Surveys.* Data disk. Washington, DC: BLS. http://www.bls.gov/nls/nlsy79.htm (accessed August 21, 2006).

―――. 2005. Industry Injury and Illness Data. Washington, DC: BLS. http://www.bls.gov/iif/oshsum.htm (accessed May 15, 2006).

Burtless, Gary. 1995. "The Employment Prospects of Welfare Recipients." In *The Work Alternative: Welfare Reform and the Realities of the Job Market,* Demetra Smith Nightingale and Robert H. Haveman, eds. Washington, DC:

Urban Institute Press, pp. 71–106.

Cappelli, Peter. 1992. "Is the 'Skills Gap' Really about Attitudes?" EQW Working Paper No. 1. Philadelphia: National Center on the Educational Quality of the Workforce, University of Pennsylvania.

————. 1993. "Are Skill Requirements Rising? Evidence from Production and Clerical Jobs." *Industrial and Labor Relations Review* 46(3): 515–530.

Card, David, and Alan B. Krueger. 1992a. "Does School Quality Matter? Returns to Education and the Characteristics of Public Schools in the United States." *Journal of Political Economy* 100(1): 1–40.

————. 1992b. "School Quality and Black-White Relative Earnings: A Direct Assessment." *Quarterly Journal of Economics* 107(1): 151–200.

Card, David, and Thomas Lemieux. 2001. "Can Falling Supply Explain the Rising Return to College for Younger Men? A Cohort-Based Analysis." *Quarterly Journal of Economics* 116(2): 705–746.

Carmichael, Lorne. 1983. "Firm-Specific Human Capital and Promotion Ladders." *Bell Journal of Economics* 14(1): 251–258.

Carrington, William J., and Bruce C. Fallick. 2001. "Do Some Workers Have Minimum Wage Careers?" *Monthly Labor Review* 124(5): 17–27.

Cawley, John, James Heckman, Lance Lochner, and Edward Vytlacil. 2000. "Understanding the Role of Cognitive Ability in Accounting for the Recent Rise in the Economic Return to Education." In *Meritocracy and Economic Inequality*, Kenneth Arrow, Samuel Bowles, and Steven Durlauf, eds. Princeton, NJ: Princeton University Press, pp. 230–265.

D'Amico, Ronald. 2005. "Short-Term Indicators and Long-Term Impacts of Job Training Programs." Paper presented at the Association for Public Policy Analysis and Management annual research conference "Understanding and Informing Policy Design," held in Washington, DC, November 3–5.

D'Amico, Ronald, and Nan L. Maxwell. 1994. "The Impact of Post-School Joblessness on Male Black-White Wage Differentials." *Industrial Relations* 33(2): 184–205.

Danziger, Sheldon, and Peter Gottschalk. 1986. "Do Rising Tides Lift All Boats? The Impact of Secular and Cyclical Changes on Poverty." *American Economic Review* 76(2): 405–410.

DeParle, Jason. 2004. *American Dream: Three Women, Ten Kids, and a Nation's Drive to End Welfare.* New York: Viking.

Devereux, Paul J. 2002. "Occupational Upgrading and the Business Cycle." *Labour* 16(3): 423–452.

Dickens, William T., and Kevin Lang. 1992. "Labor Market Segmentation Theory: Reconsidering the Evidence." NBER Working Paper No. 4087. Cambridge, MA: National Bureau of Economic Research.

Doeringer, Peter B., and Michael J. Piore. 1971. *Internal Labor Markets and*

Manpower Analysis. Lexington, MA: D.C. Heath.

Economic Development Alliance for Business (EDAB). 2001. *East Bay Indicators 2001*. Oakland, CA: EDAB. http://www.edab.org/study/East%20Bay%20Indicators%202001.pdf (accessed May 11, 2006).

Ellwood, David T. 1982. "Teenage Unemployment: Permanent Scars or Temporary Blemishes." In *The Youth Labor Market Problem: Its Nature, Causes, and Consequences,* Richard B. Freeman and David A. Wise, eds. Chicago: University of Chicago Press, pp. 349–390.

Fairris, David, and Michael Reich. 2005. "The Impacts of Living Wage Policies: Introduction to the Special Issue." *Industrial Relations* 44(1): 1–13.

Farber, Henry S. 1999. "Mobility and Stability: The Dynamics of Job Change in Labor Markets." In *The Handbook of Labor Economics*, Vol. 3, Part 2, Orley C. Ashenfelter and David Card, eds. Handbooks in Economics 5. Amsterdam: North-Holland, pp. 2439–2483.

Fernandez, Roberto M., Emillio J. Castilla, and Paul Moore. 2000. "Social Capital at Work: Networks and Employment at a Phone Center." *American Journal of Sociology* 105(5): 1288–1356.

Freeman, Richard B. 1993. "How Much Has De-Unionization Contributed to the Rise in Male Earnings Inequality?" In *Uneven Tides: Rising Inequality in America*, Sheldon Danziger and Peter Gottschalk, eds. New York: Russell Sage Foundation, pp. 133–163.

Freeman, Richard B., and Peter Gottschalk, eds. 1998. *Generating Jobs: How to Increase Demand for Less-Skilled Workers*. New York: Russell Sage Foundation.

Friedlander, Daniel, David H. Greenberg, and Philip K. Robins. 1997. "Evaluating Government Training Programs for the Economically Disadvantaged." *Journal of Economic Literature* 35(4): 1809–1855.

Gautier, Pieter A., Gerard J. van den Berg, Jan C. van Ours, and Geert Ridder. 2002. "Worker Turnover at the Firm Level and Crowding Out of Lower Educated Workers." *European Economic Review* 46(3): 523–538.

Gibbons, Robert, and Michael Waldman. 1999a. "A Theory of Wage and Promotion Dynamics Inside Firms." *Quarterly Journal of Economics* 114(4): 1321–1358.

———. 1999b. "Careers in Organizations: Theory and Evidence." In *Handbook of Labor Economics*, Vol. 3, Part 2, Orley C. Ashenfelter and David Card, eds. Handbooks in Economics 5. Amsterdam: North-Holland, pp. 2373–2437.

Gladden, Tricia, and Christopher Taber. 2000. "Wage Progression among Less Skilled Workers." In *Finding Jobs: Work and Welfare Reform*, David Card and Rebecca M. Blank, eds. New York: Russell Sage Foundation, pp. 160–192.

Goldin, Claudia, and Robert A. Margo. 1992. "The Great Compression: The Wage Structure in the United States at Mid-Century." *Quarterly Journal of Economics* 107(1): 1–34.

Gottschalk, Peter. 2005. "Can Work Alter Welfare Recipients' Beliefs?" *Journal of Policy Analysis and Management* 24(3): 485–498.

Granovetter, Mark. 1995. *Getting a Job: A Study of Contacts and Careers*, 2nd ed. Chicago: University of Chicago Press.

Greenberg, David H., Karl Ashworth, Andreas Cebulla, and Robert Walker. 2004. "Do Welfare-to-Work Programmes Work for Long?" *Fiscal Studies* 25(1): 27–53.

Greenberg, David H., Charles Michalopoulos, and Philip K. Robins. 2003. "A Meta-Analysis of Government-Sponsored Training Programs." *Industrial and Labor Relations Review* 57(1): 31–53.

Grubb, W. Norton. 1996. *Learning to Work: The Case for Reintegrating Job Training and Education*. New York: Russell Sage Foundation.

Halperin, Samuel. 1998. "Today's Forgotten Half: Still Losing Ground." In *The Forgotten Half Revisited: American Youth and Young Families, 1988–2008*, S. Halperin, ed. Washington, DC: American Youth Policy Forum, pp. 1–26.

Hamilton, Gayle, Stephen Freedman, Lisa Gennetian, Charles Michalopoulos, Johanna Walter, Diana Adams-Ciardullo, Anna Gassman-Pines, Sharon McGroder, Martha Zaslow, Jennifer Brooks, and Surjeet Ahluwalia. 2001. *How Effective Are Different Welfare-to-Work Approaches? Five-Year Adult and Child Impacts for Eleven Programs*. The National Evaluation of Welfare-to-Work Strategies Project. New York: Manpower Demonstration Research Corporation.

Handel, Michael J. 2003. "Skills Mismatch in the Labor Market." *Annual Review of Sociology* 29(2003): 135–165.

Hecker, Daniel E. 1992. "Reconciling Conflicting Data on Jobs for College Graduates." *Monthly Labor Review* 115(7): 3–12.

———. 1995. "Further Analyses of the Labor Market for College Graduates." Research Summaries. *Monthly Labor Review* 118(2): 39–41.

Heckman, James, Neil Hohmann, and Jeffrey Smith. 2000. "Substitution and Dropout Bias in Social Experiments: A Study of an Influential Social Experiment." *Quarterly Journal of Economics* 115(2): 651–694.

Holzer, Harry J. 1996. *What Employers Want: Job Prospects for Less-Educated Workers*. New York: Russell Sage Foundation.

Holzer, Harry J., and Robert J. LaLonde. 2000. "Job Change and Job Stability Among Less-Skilled Young Workers." In *Finding Jobs: Work and Welfare Reform*, David Card and Rebecca M. Blank, eds. New York: Russell Sage Foundation, pp. 125–159.

Holzer, Harry J., Julia I. Lane, and Lars Vilhuber. 2004. "Escaping Low Earnings: The Role of Employer Characteristics and Changes." *Industrial and Labor Relations Review* 57(4): 560–578.

Hoynes, Hilary W. 2000. "The Employment, Earnings, and Income of Less Skilled Workers over the Business Cycle." In *Finding Jobs: Work and Welfare Reform*, David Card and Rebecca M. Blank, eds. New York: Russell Sage Foundation, pp. 23–71.

Human Investment Research and Education (HIRE). 2006. Bay Area Longitudinal Surveys (BALS) Data. Hayward, CA: HIRE. http://www.hire.csueastbay .edu/Hire/bals.htm (accessed July 19, 2006).

Iceland, John, Kathleen Short, Thesia I. Garner, and David Johnson. 2001. "Are Children Worse Off? Evaluating Well-Being Using a New (and Improved) Measure of Poverty." *Journal of Human Resources* 36(2): 398–412.

Jasinowski, Jerry J. 2001. *The Skills Gap 2001: Manufacturers Confront Persistent Skills Shortages in an Uncertain Economy*. Washington, DC: National Association of Manufacturers, Center for Workforce Success.

Johnson, Rucker C., and Mary E. Corcoran. 2003. "The Road to Economic Self-Sufficiency: Job Quality and Job Transition Patterns after Welfare Reform." *Journal of Policy Analysis and Management* 22(4): 615–639.

Juhn, Chinhui. 1992. "Decline of Male Labor Market Participation: The Role of Declining Market Opportunities." *Quarterly Journal of Economics* 107(1): 79–122.

Juhn, Chinhui, Kevin M. Murphy, and Brooks Pierce. 1993. "Wage Inequality and the Rise in Returns to Skill." *Journal of Political Economy* 101(3): 410–442.

Juhn, Chinhui, Kevin M. Murphy, and Robert H. Topel. 1991. "Why Has the Natural Rate of Unemployment Increased over Time?" *Brookings Papers on Economic Activity* (2): 75–142.

Kahn, Lawrence M., and Stuart A. Low. 1988. "Systematic and Random Search: A Synthesis." *Journal of Human Resources* 23(1): 1–20.

Karoly, Lynn A. 1993. "The Trend in Inequality among Families, Individuals, and Workers in the United States: A Twenty-Five Year Perspective." In *Uneven Tides: Rising Inequality in America*, Sheldon Danziger and Peter Gottschalk, eds. New York: Russell Sage Foundation, pp. 19–97.

Katz, Lawrence F., and Kevin M. Murphy. 1992. "Changes in Relative Wages, 1963–1987: Supply and Demand Factors." *Quarterly Journal of Economics* 107(1): 35–78.

Kazis, Richard, and Marc S. Miller, eds. 2001. *Low-Wage Workers in the New Economy*. Washington, DC: Urban Institute.

Keane, Michael P., and Kenneth I. Wolpin. 1997. "The Career Decisions of Young Men." *Journal of Political Economy* 105(3): 473–522.

Kemple, James J. 2001. *Career Academies: Impacts on Students' Initial Transitions to Post-Secondary Education and Employment*. New York: Manpower Demonstration Research Corporation.

Kuhn, Peter, and Mikal Skuterud. 2000. "Job Search Methods: Internet versus Traditional." *Monthly Labor Review* 123(10): 3–12.

LaLonde, Robert J. 1995. "The Promise of Public Sector–Sponsored Training Programs." *Journal of Economic Perspectives* 9(2): 149–168.

Lang, Kevin, and William T. Dickens. 1988. "Neoclassical and Sociological Perspectives on Segmented Labor Markets." In *Industries, Firms, and Jobs: Sociological and Economic Approaches*, George Farkas and Paula England, eds. New York: Plenum Press, pp. 65–88.

Lazear, Edward P., and Sherwin Rosen. 1981. "Rank-Order Tournaments as Optimum Labor Contracts." *Journal of Political Economy* 89(5): 841–864.

Leigh, Duane E. 1976. "Occupational Advancement in the Late 1960s: An Indirect Test of the Dual Labor Market Hypothesis." *Journal of Human Resources* 11(2): 155–171.

Levy, Frank. 1987. *Dollars and Dreams: The Changing American Income Distribution*. New York: Russell Sage Foundation.

Levy, Frank, and Richard C. Michel. 1991. *The Economic Future of American Families: Income and Wealth Trends*. Washington, DC: Urban Institute.

Levy, Frank, and Richard J. Murnane. 1992. "U.S. Earnings Levels and Earnings Inequality: A Review of Recent Trends and Proposed Explanations." *Journal of Economic Literature* 30(3): 1333–1381.

Lillard, Lee A., and Hong W. Tan. 1992. "Private Sector Training: Who Gets It and What Are Its Effects?" In *Research in Labor Economics*, Vol. 13, Ronald G. Ehrenberg, ed. Greenwich, CN: JAI Press, pp. 1–62.

Lynch, Lisa M. 1989. "The Youth Labor Market in the Eighties: Determinants of Re-employment Probabilities for Young Men and Women." *Review of Economics and Statistics* 71(1): 37–45.

Manwaring, Tony, and Stephan Wood. 1984. "Recruitment and the Recession." *The International Journal of Social Economics* 11(1984): 49–63.

Maxfield, Myles. 1988. *Getting Hired: Characteristics Employers Prefer in Unskilled Job Applicants*. Washington, DC: Brookings Institution, Greater Washington Research Program.

Maxwell, Nan L. 2004a. "The Bay Area Longitudinal Surveys (BALS) of Firms." HIRE Center Discussion Paper D04-06-04. Hayward, CA: California State University, East Bay. http://www.hire.csueastbay.edu/hire/discpap/abstracts/D04-06-04.pdf (accessed July 20, 2006).

———. 2004b. "Describing South Hayward: Diversity along Many Dimensions." HIRE Center Report F04-01-01. Hayward, CA: California State University, East Bay. http://www.hire.csueastbay.edu/hire/discpap/

abstracts/F03-11-08.pdf (accessed July 20, 2006).

———. 2004c. "Skill Sets in the Bay Area Longitudinal Surveys (BALS) Data." HIRE Center Discussion Paper D04-06-07. Hayward, CA: California State University, East Bay. http://www.hire.csueastbay.edu/hire/discpap/abstracts/D04-06-07.pdf (accessed July 20, 2006).

———. Forthcoming. "Smoothing the Transition from School to Work: Job Skills." In *Improving School-to-Work Transitions*, David Neumark, ed. New York: Russell Sage Foundation.

McCue, Kristin. 1996. "Promotions and Wage Growth." *Journal of Labor Economics* 14(2): 175–209.

McMenamin, Terence M., Rachel Krantz, and Thomas J. Krolik. 2003. "U.S. Labor Market in 2002: Continued Weakness." *Monthly Labor Review* 126(2): 3–25.

Meyer, Robert H., and David A. Wise. 1982. "High School Preparation and Early Labor Force Experience." In *The Youth Labor Market Problem: Its Nature, Causes, and Consequences*, Richard B. Freeman and David A. Wise, eds. Chicago: University of Chicago Press, pp. 277–348.

Moss, Philip, and Chris Tilly. 2001. *Stories Employers Tell: Race, Skill, and Hiring in America*. Multi-City Study of Urban Inequality Series. New York: Russell Sage Foundation.

Munger, Frank, ed. 2002. *Laboring Below the Line: The New Ethnography of Poverty, Low-Wage Work, and Survival in the Global Economy*. New York: Russell Sage Foundation.

Murnane, Richard J., and Frank Levy. 1996. *Teaching the New Basic Skills: Principles for Educating Children to Thrive in a Changing Economy*. New York: Martin Kessler Books, Free Press.

Murnane, Richard J., John B. Willett, and Frank Levy. 1995. "The Growing Importance of Cognitive Skills in Wage Determination." *Review of Economics and Statistics* 77(2): 251–266.

Murphy, Kevin M., and Robert H. Topel. 1997. "Unemployment and Nonemployment." Papers and Proceedings of the Hundred and Fourth Annual Meeting of the American Economic Association. *American Economic Review* 87(2): 295–300.

Murphy, Kevin M., and Finis Welch. 1993. "Industrial Change and the Rising Importance of Skill." In *Uneven Tides: Rising Inequality in America*, Sheldon Danziger and Peter Gottschalk, eds. New York: Russell Sage Foundation, pp. 101–132.

National Commission on Excellence in Education. 1983. *A Nation at Risk: The Imperative for Educational Reform*. A Report to the Nation and the Secretary of Education. Washington, DC: U.S. Department of Education.

National Crosswalk Service Center (NCSC). 2006. *O*NET*. Des Moines, IA:

NCSC. http://www.xwalkcenter.org/onet51 (accessed February 6, 2006).

Neckerman, Kathryn M., and Joleen Kirschenman. 1991. "Hiring Strategies, Racial Bias, and Inner-City Workers." *Social Problems* 38(4): 433–447.

Newman, Katherine S. 1999. *No Shame in My Game: The Working Poor in the Inner City*. New York: Alfred A. Knopf.

Occupational Information Network (O*NET). 2006a. *O*NET OnLine: Skills Search*. Raleigh, NC: O*NET. http://online.onetcenter.org/skills (accessed July 20, 2006).

———. 2006b. *Abilities Questionnaire*. Raleigh, NC: O*NET. http://harvey.psyc.vt.edu/Documents/ONETabilities.pdf (accessed July 20, 2006).

———. 2006c. *Development Database—O*NET 10.0*. Raleigh, NC: O*NET. http://www.onetcenter.org/dev_db.html (accessed August 22, 2006).

O'Neil, Harold F., Jr., Keith Allred, and Eva L. Baker. 1997. "Review of Workforce Readiness Theoretical Frameworks." In *Workforce Readiness: Competencies and Assessment*. Harold F. O'Neil Jr., ed. Mahwah, NJ: Lawrence Erlbaum Associates, pp. 3–26.

Osberg, Lars. 1993. "Fishing in Different Pools: Job-Search Strategies and Job-Finding Success in Canada in the Early 1980s." *Journal of Labor Economics* 11(2): 348–386.

Osterman, Paul. 1980. *Getting Started: The Youth Labor Market*. Cambridge, MA: MIT Press.

Pergamit, Michael R., and Jonathan R. Veum. 1999. "What is a Promotion?" *Industrial and Labor Relations Review* 52(4): 581–601.

Piore, Michael J. 1983. "Labor Market Segmentation: To What Paradigm Does It Belong?" *American Economic Review* 73(2): 249–253.

Prendergast, Canice. 1993. "The Role of Promotion in Inducing Specific Human Capital Acquisition." *Quarterly Journal of Economics* 108(2): 523–534.

Pryor, Frederic L., and David L. Schaffer. 1999. *Who's Not Working and Why: Employment, Cognitive Skills, Wages, and the Changing U.S. Labor Market*. Cambridge: Cambridge University Press.

Rangarajan, Anu. 2001. "Staying On, Moving Up: Strategies to Help Entry-Level Workers Retain Employment and Advance in Their Jobs." In *Low-Wage Workers in the New Economy*, Richard Kazis and Marc S. Miller, eds. Washington, DC: Urban Institute, pp. 91–110.

Rebitzer, James B., and Lowell J. Taylor. 1991. "A Model of Dual Labor Markets When Product Demand is Uncertain." *Quarterly Journal of Economics* 106(4): 1373–1383.

Revenga, Ana L. 1992. "Exporting Jobs? The Impact of Import Competition on Employment and Wages in U.S. Manufacturing." *Quarterly Journal of Economics* 107(1): 255–284.

Rodecker, Jared. 2004. *Common Training Occupations and Projected Openings: Over-Training and Under-Training of WIA Program Participants.* Oakland, CA: Social Policy Research Associates.

Rosen, Sherwin. 1986. "Prizes and Incentives in Elimination Tournaments." *American Economic Review* 76(4): 701–715.

Rosenbaum, James. 2001. *Beyond College for All: Career Paths for the Forgotten Half.* The American Sociological Association's Rose Series in Sociology. New York: Russell Sage Foundation.

Royalty, Anne Beeson. 1998. "Job-to-Job and Job-to-Nonemployment Turnover by Gender and Educational Level." *Journal of Labor Economics* 16(2): 392–443.

Saint-Paul, Gilles. 1997. *Dual Labor Markets: A Macroeconomic Perspective.* Cambridge, MA: MIT Press.

Salop, Steven C. 1979. "A Model of the Natural Rate of Unemployment." *American Economic Review* 69(1): 117–125.

Sawicky, Max B., ed. 1999. *The End of Welfare? Consequences of Federal Devolution for the Nation.* Armonk, NY: M.E. Sharpe.

Shapiro, Carl, and Joseph E. Stiglitz. 1984. "Equilibrium Unemployment as a Worker Discipline Device." *American Economic Review* 74(3): 433–444.

Shipler, David K. 2004. *The Working Poor: Invisible in America.* New York: Alfred A. Knopf.

Snyder, Thomas D., Alexandra G. Tan, and Charlene M. Hoffman. 2004. *Digest of Education Statistics, 2003.* Washington, DC: U.S. Department of Education, National Center for Education Statistics. http://nces.ed.gov/programs/digest/d03/ (accessed May 12, 2006).

Stoft, Steven. 1982. "Cheat-Threat Theory: An Explanation of Involuntary Unemployment." Unpublished manuscript. Boston, MA: Boston University.

Teulings, Coen N. 1995. "The Wage Distribution in a Model of the Assignment of Skills to Jobs." *Journal of Political Economy* 103(2): 280–315.

Teulings, Coen N., and Marc A. Koopmanschap. 1989. "An Econometric Model of Crowding Out of Lower Education Levels." *European Economic Review* 33(8): 1653–1664.

Tyler, John H., Richard J. Murnane, and John B. Willett. 2000. "Do the Cognitive Skills of School Dropouts Matter in the Labor Market?" *Journal of Human Resources* 35(4): 748–754.

U.S. Census Bureau. 2003a. *Statistical Abstract of the United States 2002: The National Data Book.* 122nd ed. Washington, DC: U.S. Census Bureau.

———. 2003b. *American FactFinder.* Washington, DC: U.S. Census Bureau. http://factfinder.census.gov/home/saff/main.html?_lang=en (accessed May 15, 2006).

———. 2003c. *Census 2000 Public Use Microdata Sample (PUMS), Census of the Population and Housing.* Data disk. Washington, DC: U.S. Census Bureau. http://www.census.gov/support/PUMSdata.html (accessed June 27, 2006).

U.S. Department of Labor (USDOL), Employment and Training Administration (ETA). 2004. *PY 2002 Public Use WIASRD.* Data disk issued April 7. Washington, DC: USDOL, ETA. http://www.doleta.gov/performance/Reporting/ wiasrd.cfm (accessed June 27, 2006).

————. 2005. *Workforce System Results: Third Quarter, Program Year 2004; Second Quarter, Fiscal Year 2005; January 1–March 31, 2005.* Washington, DC: USDOL, ETA. http://www.doleta.gov/Performance/results/Edition _03_31_05.pdf (accessed May 15, 2006).

————. 2006. *Occupational Information Network Resource Center.* Washington, DC: USDOL, ETA. http://www.onetcenter.org (accessed June 26, 2006).

van Ours, Jan C., and Geert Ridder. 1995. "Job Matching and Job Competition: Are Lower Educated Workers at the Back of the Job Queues?" *European Economic Review* 39(9): 1717–1731.

Vickers, Margaret. 1995. "Employer Participation in School-to-Work Programs: The Changing Situation in Europe." In *Learning to Work: Employer Involvement in School-to-Work Transition Programs,* Thomas R. Bailey, ed. Brookings Dialogues on Public Policy. Washington, DC: Brookings Institution, pp. 26–44.

Weiss, Andrew. 1980. "Job Queues and Layoffs in Labor Markets with Flexible Wages." *Journal of Political Economy* 88(3): 526–538.

————. 1990. *Efficiency Wages: Models of Unemployment, Layoffs, and Wage Dispersion.* Princeton, NJ: Princeton University Press.

Woodbury, Stephen A. 1979. "Methodological Controversy in Labor Economics." *Journal of Economic Issues* 13(4): 933–955.

Workforce Investment Act of 1998 (WIA). 1998. HR 1385. 105th Cong., 2nd sess. *Congressional Record* 144.

Zemsky, Robert. 1994. *What Employers Want: Employer Perspectives on Youth, the Youth Labor Market, and Prospects for a National System of Youth Apprenticeships.* Philadelphia: University of Pennsylvania, National Center on the Educational Quality of the Workforce.

Zito, Kelly. 2003. "Eastward Ho: Bay Area Prices Drive Buyers to Central Valley." *San Francisco Chronicle,* February 16, G:1.

The Author

Nan L. Maxwell is a professor and chair of the Department of Economics and the executive director of the Human Investment Research and Education (HIRE) Center at California State University, East Bay. Her research expertise focuses on the areas of improving employment and educational opportunities for disadvantaged workers and at-risk youth, easing the transition from school to work, assessing the impact of basic skills on labor market opportunities, and evaluating alternative educational strategies. She has published over 35 journal articles or book chapters in the areas of labor market operations and human capital, demographic influences on labor market outcomes, and educational policies and strategies. She has authored two previous books, *Income Inequality in the United States, 1947–1985* (Greenwood Press, 1990) and *High School Career Academies: A Pathway to Educational Reform in Urban Schools?* (with Victor Rubin, W.E. Upjohn Institute, 2000)

Maxwell earned a bachelor of science degree from the University of Texas, a master of science and a master of labor and human resources degree from Ohio State University, and a PhD in economics from Florida State University. As a visiting scholar, she spent three years at the Institute of Urban and Regional Development and one year at the National Center for Research in Vocational Education, both at the University of California, Berkeley. She has also held a visiting professorship at the Academy of National Economy in Moscow.

Index

The italic letters *n* and *t* following a page number indicate that the subject information of the heading is within a note or table, respectively, on that page.

About the Institute

The W.E. Upjohn Institute for Employment Research is a nonprofit research organization devoted to finding and promoting solutions to employment-related problems at the national, state, and local levels. It is an activity of the W.E. Upjohn Unemployment Trustee Corporation, which was established in 1932 to administer a fund set aside by Dr. W.E. Upjohn, founder of The Upjohn Company, to seek ways to counteract the loss of employment income during economic downturns.

The Institute is funded largely by income from the W.E. Upjohn Unemployment Trust, supplemented by outside grants, contracts, and sales of publications. Activities of the Institute comprise the following elements: 1) a research program conducted by a resident staff of professional social scientists; 2) a competitive grant program, which expands and complements the internal research program by providing financial support to researchers outside the Institute; 3) a publications program, which provides the major vehicle for disseminating the research of staff and grantees, as well as other selected works in the field; and 4) an Employment Management Services division, which manages most of the publicly funded employment and training programs in the local area.

The broad objectives of the Institute's research, grant, and publication programs are to 1) promote scholarship and experimentation on issues of public and private employment and unemployment policy, and 2) make knowledge and scholarship relevant and useful to policymakers in their pursuit of solutions to employment and unemployment problems.

Current areas of concentration for these programs include causes, consequences, and measures to alleviate unemployment; social insurance and income maintenance programs; compensation; workforce quality; work arrangements; family labor issues; labor-management relations; and regional economic development and local labor markets.